Successful Study

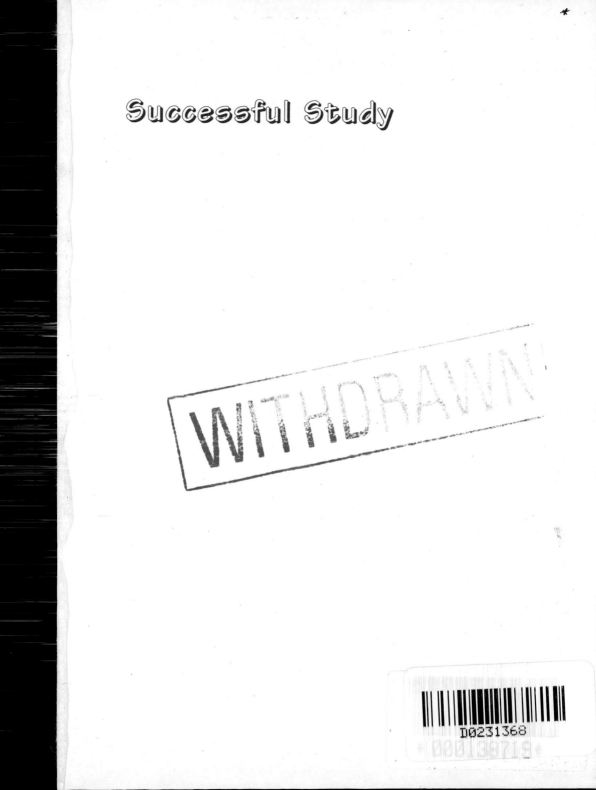

Successful Study

THE ESSENTIAL SKILLS

Prashant Shah

Prashant Shah currently works in Strategic Services
in Andersen Consulting, London.

Letts

Letts Educational
Aldine Place
LONDON
W12 8AW
Tel: 0181-740 2268
Fax: 0181-743 8451
e-mail: he@lettsed.co.uk

Acknowledgements

Special thanks to my father, Shirish Becharlal Shah, for criticising and thoroughly correcting multiple drafts of this book, to my mother, Sharmista Shah, and to my brother, Sunil Shah, for their encouragement. Many thanks are due to Greg Wilson, whose cartoons have added a light-hearted touch to this book. I owe a very special debt of gratitude to Andrew Willis, Indra Marajh, John Odell, Alpa Shah, Mark Sandford, Robin Murdoch, Sona Shah, Harjinder Kaur, and Preeti Shah for having kindly given their time to offer feedback on earlier drafts. Thanks also to Jon Allan, Brigitte Lee, Kumud Shah, Rachel Jackson, Talib Ali, Des Sutton, Chris Bowsher, Paul Turner, and Chris Henderson for their help and comments. Lastly, special thanks are also due to the team from Letts, including Nathalie Manners and Ed Peppitt, for their very strong support during the development of this book.

A CIP catalogue record for this book can be obtained from the British Library

ISBN 1-85805-357-9

Text and illustrations concept copyright Prashant Shah © 1998
Illustrations copyright BPP (Letts Educational) Ltd © 1998
Cartoon concept copyright Greg Wilson © 1998

Designed and typeset by Ian Foulis Associates
Cartoons by Greg Wilson

Printed and bound in Great Britain by Progressive Printing (UK) Ltd, Leigh on Sea, Essex

Summary of Chapters

TOTAL LEARNING

1. Introduction: Improve now
2. Think about your life strategy
3. Know your degree
4. Be organised
5. Make planning easy
6. Planning courseworks and exam reviews
7. Concurrent revision
8. Prepare easy-to-learn revision notes using spider-diagrams
9. Use mnemonics to improve memory during exams
10. Rapid revision
11. The exam
12. Projects and dissertations

Contents

"...a living mind is a mind that has no centre and therefore no space or time. Such a mind is limitless and that is the only truth, that is the only reality."

J. Krishnamurti[1]

Learning – the art and science of acquiring knowledge – is vital in today's society. Knowledge, its recall and application, can shape your ability to tackle present demands and open doors to future exciting opportunities. Learning effectively is a skill that we need to know throughout our lives, but it is rarely properly taught.

This book describes the essential skills required to replace poor learning techniques at degree level. Each chapter forms an element of the approach called **Total Learning**, in which the key aspects of learning that affect your performance are examined.

The skills provided in this book will equip you with the confidence to redefine and exceed your own potential, and help you to develop your own new set of learning skills. The aim of this book is for you to do the seemingly impossible: to achieve higher grades through less effort and to have a lot more spare time to do the other things you really should be enjoying at college/university.

[1] J. Krishnamurti, *Freedom from the Known*, ed. Mary Lutyens (BI Publications PVT Ltd, 1969; reprinted 1986), p. 110.

Introduction

Learn the essential skills for successful study and you will be certain to make the most of your time at college/university

Introduction

Warning: Improve your technique now or spend more time studying than you have to!

Would you like to go through college/university and achieve good grades in your coursework and exams, but never have to miss out on a lively evening with your friends? Unless you prefer studying to the pleasures of college/university life, you should ask yourself: 'What recent changes have I made to my learning technique? When did I last experiment with a different way of learning?'

It is very important to challenge the effectiveness of your learning technique, to improve on it, and to continue to adjust it for different subjects and situations. Many of us are prepared to listen to suggestions pertaining to our learning skills, but we actually get far too little constructive help. Students are often cagey about sharing their most favoured secret shortcuts with other students. Our parents teach us many things, but how many of them teach us to learn effectively? Unfortunately, many colleges/universities are also guilty of not giving us sufficient training in the study skills we really need.

In spite of that, most of us will have stumbled into a learning approach that worked reasonably well for the exams we took to gain entry into college/university. Once there, the pressures on your time, the way in which information is presented and subjects assessed will certainly be very different. You will need to change your learning skills to make the most of your valuable time at college/university.

Technique, drive, intelligence and confidence

I have sat through countless lectures unashamedly day-dreaming (or sleeping) while other beings of superior intelligence appeared to be absorbing pearls of wisdom first time around. Luckily for me, intelligence is only one of the ingredients necessary for degree success. If you develop the right learning skills, the apparent obstacle of not having an amazingly high level of intelligence can be readily overcome.

You do not have to be of more than average intelligence to get fantastic results at university

I believe that the four key ingredients of degree success are: technique, drive, intelligence and confidence. But without a doubt it is technique that brings out the best of the other three ingredients. When you sharpen up your learning technique, you can revitalise your drive to learn and uncover previously untapped stores of mental brilliance. The result is that you become more confident of your own abilities as you move closer to achieving your maximum possible potential (see Figure 1.1).

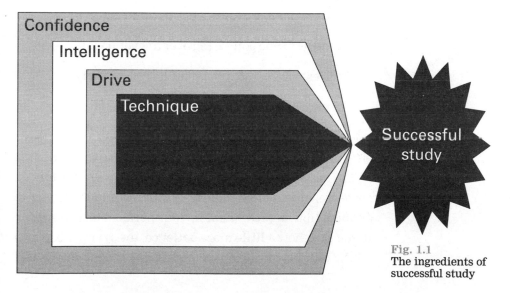

Fig. 1.1
The ingredients of successful study

About this book

This book describes a workable approach to improving your performance called **Total Learning**. Although there are some new concepts, you will find that most of the skills are based on common-sense principles. It is an approach that will produce results because you will:

✔ Develop a zest to learn you never thought you had.

✔ Develop the skills that *really* enhance your performance in courseworks and exams.

✔ Feel as if you have a secret learning power.

I have tutored students who have astonished themselves at the upturn in their own performance. When you are armed with the essential skills, you should also be able to:

✔ Waste little effort (wasted effort is a disaster).

✔ Understand better the subjects you once found difficult to grasp.

✔ Outperform students who are very intelligent or who have real in-depth knowledge of a subject.

✔ Spend less time pondering over a set of books.

✔ Feel less sick at the thought of having to study.

✔ Achieve higher grades in courseworks and examinations.

Now let us consider how you might choose to tackle this book. It is perfectly acceptable to read chapters selectively, since even the smallest change in your technique can lead to an incredible improvement in your performance. However, if you can show a little more patience, the synergy between all the different skills of the Total Learning approach will begin to develop and your ability to learn will reach new, previously unimagined heights.

As a final note to this chapter, when you are considering a change to the way you study you should carefully observe the following three points:

✔ Always try out the changes which are the easiest to achieve first.

✔ Do not force changes into your way of working unless they feel comfortable.

✔ Avoid drastic changes just before a major exam.

SUMMARY

Major emphasis is currently being placed on the grade you achieve in your degree. Your learning technique will therefore become increasingly important as it becomes more vital to make use of your opportunity at college/university. These improvements could mean the difference between a 2:2 and a 2:1 or a 2:1 and a 1st. While the differences between a 2:1 and a 2:2 may be negligible in terms of marks, the possible effects on a planned career may be quite significant.

Lastly, recognition of the fact that you have **attained** a degree can never be taken away from you. It doesn't have an expiry date and you can't gamble it away. You can lose a job and eventually your youthful good looks, but you can't lose your education.

You are now in a position to...

Consider the benefits of a Total Learning approach at college/university

Think about the effect that technique has on the three other ingredients of successful study

Realise how urgently you need to improve your technique

Think About Your Life Strategy

2

It is critical to clarify what you want to do in the future, prioritise your objectives for next year, and decide what level of success you desire in your degree

Clarify Your Motivations

What do you want to do in the future?

Ask yourself why you want to complete a degree. Perhaps your motivation is to start up a business, research a subject to a higher level, or to gain the appropriate entry standards for a career. Whatever your motivation, try to specify it.

You may be tempted to skip over such thoughts. But do spend a few moments taking stock of your current situation and your long-term goals. It is important for you to know how your intended actions today, this week or this year will relate to what you want to do in the future.

Prioritise your objectives

Decide on the 'must achieve' objectives during your degree

You may have many loosely defined objectives prior to the start of each year. However, it will not hurt to list them all down. Then decide which ones you **must achieve** and which ones would be **nice to achieve**. Be realistic and cut the 'must achieve' objectives down to the minimum. By focusing on a narrower set of 'must achieve' objectives, you are more likely to achieve them.

How many times have grandiose plans made at the beginning of the year been steadily eroded? It is very important actually to carry out what you set out to achieve. Failure to realise your 'must achieve' objectives can be damaging to your confidence.

How to Sketch Your Life Strategy

If you have clarified what you want to do in the future and prioritised your objectives for next year into 'must achieve' and 'nice to achieve' objectives, add to this your target grade and you now have the three elements that make up a life strategy. The target grade and your objectives for next year should align with your future plans.

A life strategy is the relationship of these three elements over time. The best way to test whether your life strategy 'fits together' is in the form of a simple sketch (see Figure 2.1) If you understand exactly how your degree fits into your life, you will know how to harness your motivation and make the difficult choices on how to spend your time.

Take five minutes to sketch out your life strategy

The following list provides a few extra suggestions to help you to develop your own life strategy sketch:

✓ Include a simple timescale to outline the order of events.

✓ Identify the major turning points in your life and anticipate how they might affect setting your target grade.

✓ Add more detail to the sketch to explain/justify your target grade.

✓ Clearly emphasise 'must achieve' objectives during your degree and beyond.

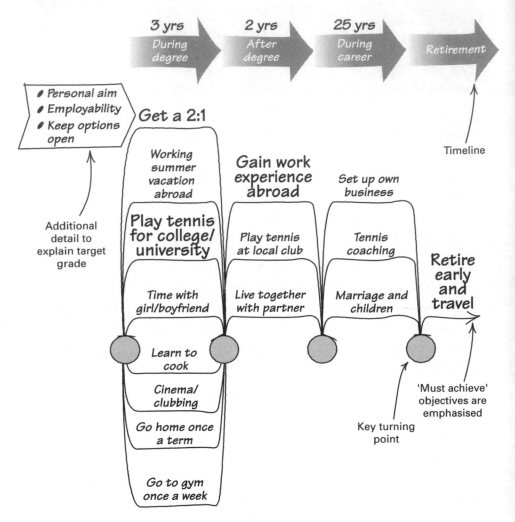

Fig. 2.1
Life strategy: an example

The future is unpredictable and changes of plan will be inevitable as your circumstances and aspirations change. However, your life strategy sketch will encourage you to be realistic about your expectations during your degree, without constraining what is possible. It may even open up your current thinking to consider other possibilities or missed opportunities.

SUMMARY

You are now in a position to...

Think about what you want to do in the future

Separate 'must achieve' objectives from 'nice to achieve' objectives

Fix your target grade

Sketch out your life strategy

Know Your Degree

Lay solid preparatory foundations before each academic year. Make sure you find out everything you need to know about the structure, operation, options, lecturers and particular needs of your degree

Choosing Your Subject Options

At the beginning of the year nearly all students are faced with a number of difficult subject choice dilemmas. Take the trouble to discover more about the subjects you intend to study before choosing them. The mix of subjects can make life very easy or unnecessarily difficult.

However, only one thing really matters when evaluating your subject options, and that is to choose the mix of subjects that will result in the best grades for the least amount of work. Consider the following points:

✔ Do what you enjoy and find interesting. You will have to dig deep into your reserves of motivation many times during the year to do well in a subject. But take care: interesting subjects can sometimes lose their appeal if you look likely to score a low grade.

✔ Pick a subject which overlaps with something you have come across before. This will help you break into the subject much more quickly.

✔ Cluster your subject options. If the chosen subjects are closely related, your overall understanding of all of the subjects will be deepened.

✔ Certain lecturers will respond more generously to your style of work or requests for help.

✔ Know which lecturers/subjects will result in a lower overall volume of work.

Avoid choosing a subject just because it might be useful in a planned career. If it means extra work, is boring or difficult, it might result in a low score. Remember, it is the grade you achieve, not necessarily the specific mix of subjects, which will be more important to you in your career. Bear in mind that:

✔ Employers will look unfavourably at bad grades.

✔ Your choice of career may change several times during your lifetime.

✔ A good company will provide you with the specific training you need for a job.

Know Your Lecturers

Do not neglect your lecturers. Treat their expectations of your work with care. You should aim to tailor every one of your assignments or exam answers to meet the individual styles of each of your lecturers. Failure to do so could result in the loss of potentially easy marks.

Every coursework, exam question or dissertation is usually marked by one person. Despite lecturers' best attempts to standardise marking, what is expected will vary from lecturer to lecturer. It is too late to find out after the marking has been done.

Lecturers are a source of invaluable tips on how to tackle coursework and exams. With a little probing they can often be very helpful. Ask simple open-ended questions in class, or better, after lectures (lecturers are a little more open in a one-to-one). You may also find out some useful information from last year's students and from past work that has been marked.

Often, the things a lecturer looks for are reassuringly simple; some lecturers like you to put in your own thinking; some lecturers emphasise (and are swayed by) good presentation, while others appreciate a focus on the basics, and so on. If it is a coursework, project or an essay, do ask about the presentation, structure and the essential areas to cover etc., as this will ensure that you waste as little effort as possible.

In particular, listen out for and write down tips given at the beginning and end of the lecture. Sometimes the lecture is accompanied by statements such as 'this is what you need to know' and 'this is background'. Make sure you clearly highlight or write down, at the time, if a tip is given, as you may not remember all of the details later on.

One final point. If a grade in a subject is important to you, tell your lecturer. Then let them tell you exactly what they expect, for example from a 2:1 or a 1st. This information should not be and is not classified. Such a conversation lays out a 'clear statement of aims' and provides highly valuable guidance and structure on how to ensure that your efforts are made to meet the specific requirements of that lecturer.

Know Your Course

Know the dates of your exams and coursework deadlines

Find out for certain when your exams will occur. If you know beforehand the fixed exam dates you are working towards, you will focus your efforts more effectively.

Coursework deadlines are usually vague in course brochures and are often subject to change. So try to find out for yourself exactly how many courseworks (essays, labs, presentations, etc.) you have to do, and exactly when you must complete them. Mark the time you expect each one to take in your diary, and you will find large chunks of your time available for work during the term rapidly disappearing! You will then begin to realise how little time you actually have to prepare and learn revision notes for the exams. Planning and scheduling are covered in more detail in Chapters 5 and 6.

Obtain past exam papers early

Exam papers are available from university bookshops, libraries, the department administration or the lecturers themselves. Try to obtain at least three years' worth of past papers. However, beware of questions that featured in last year's paper but will no longer appear in the future owing to changes in the syllabus.

At first the questions will appear incomprehensible since you have not yet completed the course. Don't be alarmed, as you will master it. Nevertheless, it is good to get that shock out of the way as soon as you can.

Get familiar with the style and structure of the paper immediately

31

Identify groups of questions from past papers that are very similar and check these groups of questions against a course brochure. Such preliminary analysis of past papers and grouping of similar questions will increase your awareness of the material provided during the lecture. You will also feel much more confident when carrying out that annual student gamble of 'question spotting'.

Know the allocation of marks and allocate the appropriate effort

Allocate effort in proportion to the split of marks between coursework and exams. A coursework may account for only 20 per cent of the total available marks on a subject, but it is unlikely that your effort will actually be allocated in this proportion. The coursework is usually submitted well in advance of the exam, when there is not a lot of pressure. The examination preparation will often get crushed into the day before the exam (when there is a lot of pressure). So place a ceiling on the amount of time you devote to coursework which is worth only a small number of marks. Coursework can 'suck up' time; you have been warned.

Allocate effort to the bulk of your marks

Though time should be allocated in proportion to the available marks for courseworks, there are instances where exceptions should be granted. For example, you will often find that when you are doing a coursework, you are under-taking a learning curve which will save you time when preparing your revision notes for the examination.

Getting books

Lecturers have a tendency to recommend a lot of books which could cost a fortune, while resources in most universities are in short supply. Therefore, speak to students who did your course last year to find out which books are really essential and then buy them as soon as possible.

Investment in books is well worth the money

When time is short and you urgently need to refer to something you do not understand, you don't want to be chasing around a bookshop, library or a friend to find that important book. If you have the book quickly to hand, you can learn faster. Money spent on educating yourself to achieve your desired grade is rarely money unwisely spent.

Past students can give you priceless help

Whatever it takes, get hold of students who have done your course and discuss all aspects of the course with them. They can provide you with:

✔ Copies of essays, marks and feedback from previous lecturers.

✔ Cheap books, now no longer required.

✔ Methods for tackling difficult lecturers!

If you have a range of subjects to choose from, discuss it with them. If possible, flick through a complete set of their lecture notes to see if it is a subject you like. A subject can seem quite appealing from a course brochure, but the reality may be disappointing. A word of warning: listen to these opinions, but always *trust your own instincts*.

Be ready for the special revision classes

Some lecturers hold a one-off revision class in the days before the exam. You are likely to get very little notice if and when it occurs because this special class is usually a response to student demand. Unsurprisingly, such reviews will be very close to other exams (the lecturer will not care if a review of their subject takes place the day before another exam).

Don't get caught out by last-minute revision sessions

To benefit from the level of discussion, make sure you have reviewed the relevant material for these classes prior to attendance. Therefore, it is important to begin your overall programme of preparing and learning revision notes early. If you have covered these areas well in advance, you will be able to take advantage of such a review and steer the discussion of material in the class to the areas in which you personally need most help.

Leave your revision effort to the last minute and you will not have time to attend. Avoid missing a revision class at all costs. It is at this time that lecturers are at their most generous in giving away clues to the questions on the exam paper.

SUMMARY

You are now in a position to...

Collect helpful shortcuts and information about your course from past papers, course brochures, departmental administrators, last year's students and friendly lecturers

Be

Organised

4

Organise yourself and your work to ensure that your study time is spent as usefully as it should be

Getting Out of Bed

To get a good working start to the day you first have to get out of bed

For me, getting up in the morning is a real problem. Often half-days are lost because of bad starts, and the feeling that nothing has been achieved persists for the rest of the day. I therefore sleep late, and the same thing happens all over again. So, to try to get up early, I resorted to the following (desperate) measures. You may also find them useful!

✔ Put your alarm clock on the other side of the room so that you have to get out of bed to switch it off. Avoid walking straight back to bed and falling asleep again.

✔ Go to bed at a certain time – no matter what the excuse.

✔ Put a 'get up you lazy *?*+*?!**' sign on the snooze button of your alarm clock.

✔ Drink a lot of water before you go to bed so your bladder is bursting first thing in the morning.

✔ Use more than one alarm clock.

Finding the Right Time in the Day (or Year) to Study

Assess your time-sponges

It is essential that the time you planned to study goes as smoothly as you need it to. For this to happen, you need to be alert and anticipate potential **time-sponges**. These are both non-study and study-related activities which prevent you from achieving a set task or which cause wider havoc with your revision effort. Characteristics of time-sponges include:

You may have to be inventive to find and fix a few silent study hours into your routine

- ✔ Activities that always go on much longer than you planned.

- ✔ Activities that have the habit of cropping up when available time is very scarce.

- ✔ Activities that you forgot about or the lecturer forgot to tell you about.

- ✔ Times of the day, or events in the year, when there are so many natural distractions that there is no point in planning to work at this time.

An example of a study-related time-sponge is a project presentation. To prepare the presentation material and practise it **always** takes longer than you expect. Furthermore, you will be told at the last minute that it is to occur during a week that you had carefully allocated for panic revision.

You have three alternatives when confronted with a time-sponge:

✔ Adjust the time at which you study around the time-sponge. It does not actually matter when in the day (or night) or time of the year you actually choose to do your work.

✔ Move up a gear in your determination and work through it.

✔ Put into action a plan for dealing with the unexpected (we will return to this in more detail in Chapter 5).

Avoid planning to work at times when you risk getting sucked into doing something else

Night-owls

During the year there are times when there are no lectures to attend and there is a tremendous amount of work to be done, i.e. during inter-term holidays or during exam leave. But for one reason or another, **nothing** gets done when you work during the day. This is not surprising when all the possible distractions are considered. A night shift offers a possible solution.

For example, if you are at home during the Christmas holidays, you might choose to work after midnight (providing you have not had too wild a night out) and finish between 4am and 6am. You can still make it up for a very late lunch. Working after midnight at home during Christmas has many advantages:

✔ Complete peace and quiet.

✔ Everyone else is tucked up in bed.

✔ There is nothing worthwhile on the television.

✔ Not much chance of any phone calls.

✔ Can work on the spacious dining table.

- ✔ Access to the fridge and the kitchen.

- ✔ Go out in the evening with friends.

- ✔ Relax at home or complete the daily chores in the afternoon.

The early-bird

If you are disciplined enough to get to bed early (or survive with less sleep), try scheduling 45 to 90 minutes of study before lectures begin in the morning. The thought that you have given up precious sleeping time is often enough to motivate you to work intensely during that very quiet time of the day.

Slow starts in the morning

Even if you manage to get up early in the morning, it does not always translate into an early start. This can be avoided by planning in advance what you intend to do that morning. Alternatively, if you are under serious time pressure, roll straight out of bed and into a short session before getting ready and having breakfast. These two delayed activities will then fill the first break you have planned for the morning.

During the Christmas and Easter vacations

Be warned that these vacations are often completely lost to non-study-related activities. This is because the problem of not having a quiet study time is very common during the Christmas and Easter breaks. The vital Christmas break is a chance for you to catch up on the oversocialising of the first term and to get to grips with the next term before it starts.

Apart from a few well-chosen days, plan a minimum task every day. As will be discussed in Chapter 5, even if it is only a couple of hours of study, you'll feel as if you are doing something positive. These are usually quite long holidays and it is wonderfully satisfying to begin the second term in control of your work.

Choosing the Right Place for Study

Choose a quiet place for study

There are three things you should look for when choosing the right place to study: peace, quiet and tranquillity. You will spend a lot less time studying and a lot more time out with friends if you are able to study in silence.

Working in a silent and comfortable environment will ensure that you can finish tasks more quickly

Your bedroom can sometimes be a very dangerous place to work:

✓ It requires endless tidying up when there is work to be done.

✓ A continuous stream of friends will visit, promising you wild merrymaking and debauchery on the evening before an important deadline.

✓ Bedrooms sometimes have televisions in them. From a one-time addict and sufferer of the occasional relapse, be sure to lock up your television, or unplug it and put it in a corner of the room so you switch it on only as the exception rather than the rule. If you want to watch television try to get into the habit of watching it outside your normal place of study.

✓ Music is a normal part of the study routine for many people. Unless it is a low-intensity study activity, e.g. filing your notes, try to avoid it. You will notice the difference.

If you get bored working in your bedroom, rotate your study area, e.g. mornings in the bedroom, afternoons and evenings in the library. This will help you to fix your mind on what you need to achieve in the morning or afternoon session. Furthermore, a change of setting can be refreshing (so can a change in the type of study).

A library off-campus or in town can be a helpful alternative when something really must get done. Your friends in your residence or house will not know how to get in contact with you and you can avoid the inevitable socialising that takes place at your main university library. If the library is in town, it also gives you a chance to wander around shops during a break. This is great for taking your mind off work and it shouldn't permanently distract you.

If a lack of a regular quiet study area is a problem for you, find out about a library in another department. There are also plenty of research labs etc. to which lecturers may let you have access. They can be particularly quiet during the evenings and therefore well suited to intense study.

In summary, take the initiative to find somewhere quiet to work, either by rearranging the place of study or the time of study. When you really need to get work done, avoid working in places at times where people might find you and tempt you to do something else.

Be comfortable in your place of study

There are a few things you can do to make your working environment more comfortable when studying. This will help you to maintain your studying stamina.

✔ Use a reading stand to avoid having to lean over your books.

✔ Raise the angle at which you write. It will have the effect of reducing tension in your neck (see Figure 4.1).

✔ Open a window if you can and let in some fresh air.

✔ Work near a window which is preferably to the left or right of your desk. A window directly in front of you might be too much of a distraction.

✔ Use chairs with good back support and avoid chairs that allow you to slouch.

✔ Put a watch or small clock in your line of sight during study; it will serve as a reminder of how much time you have left until your next break.

✔ If you are working long hours on a computer, give your eyes a rest by frequently looking away from the screen.

✔ Where possible, study in a large room. It is worth fighting for a large room with the accommodation administrator or your housemates if you live in a shared house.

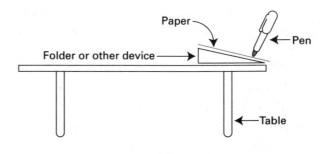

Fig. 4.1
Writing at an
angle

44

Organising Your Notes and Files

Keep your paper under control

During the year you will be inundated with paper: lecture notes, photocopies of background reading, revision notes, exam papers, etc. Rapid access to all the essential information when studying is very important and it can be extremely annoying if you are not able to find something at a critical time. Moreover, wading through masses of paper is a terrible waste of time.

A well-organised set of notes neatly filed away until you need them will encourage you to believe that you have some control over your material. There are a few simple things you can do to make things easier for yourself:

✔ Label each leaf of your lecture notes with your name, date, subject and the number sequence. When the end-of-term trading (and photocopying) of lecture notes takes place you will be glad you did this.

✔ Have a smallish day-folder you can carry with you which contains all your subjects clearly labelled. Empty it into a larger folder preferably on a weekly basis.

✔ Use an in-tray to keep other useful papers together until you are ready to file them.

✔ Keep a separate file for your revision notes as you prepare them. This will be the only file you will need for the final stages of revision.

Keep your paper-work immaculately organised, filed and labelled to avoid crisis management and to ensure lightning quick access to important information

Do not underestimate the benefits of being an excellent secretary

In summary, maintain a beautiful filing system and be proud of it. Scrupulously label all your files, folders and file dividers. Explore the organisation of your material in different ways until you find an approach that suits you, then keep a large supply of those filing materials.

Have a detailed filing system for courseworks and projects

For courseworks and project work an effective filing system is vital. Don't be shy about using file dividers to categorise the material to a very high level of detail. You are not required to remember anything when submitting courseworks or project work but to apply the information you have in hand. If you have all the various sub-categories of information relating to a coursework or project neatly filed, you are effectively extending your powers of recall without remembering a thing. The end result will be a coursework or project that is very detailed and extremely well researched.

Post-it notes

Post-it notes are amazingly versatile. Keep them in different colours and sizes

Whenever you study have a plentiful supply of post-it notes in different colours and sizes. Post-it notes are essential for referring back to pages of a book or article for quick reference. If you know that you can refer to something quickly, you are more likely to look at it. If it meant searching through tables of contents or indexes to try to find a diagram, you would probably not bother. In brief, post-it notes are incredibly useful because they can be used:

✔ As a reminder.

✔ When you need to capture a wild and creative thought.

✔ When it is helpful to organise or rearrange your thoughts on a large surface such as a wall.

✔ As a low-cost replacement for file dividers.

✔ As a supplement to file dividers. You can sub-categorise a folder of information in more detail if you stagger the post-it notes along the top or bottom edge of selected notes, articles or documents.

✔ If there are many useful pages of text or diagrams required for quick reference within a single book. Mark clearly on the post-it note what it refers to, then stick the post-it note on any edge of the book. This is preferable to turning the corners of a page (see Figure 4.2).

Fig. 4.2
Application of post-it notes to a textbook

Motivational Messages

The effects of these messages are subtle but effective. It does not hurt to remind yourself on a daily basis what your key motivations are, and in some of the darker hours of your degree they remind you just why on earth you are devoting painful hours to work when you would like to be doing other things. Messages can be written on post-it notes and placed conveniently on the wall above the desk of the room in which you work.

The message may include your reasons for doing the degree based upon your life strategy, perhaps even the name of the company you particularly wish to work for, or the destination of a holiday you planned as a reward to yourself. Alternatively, the messages might even include reprimands not to slack off and reminders to stay on top of your work. But chiefly, the most highly effective means of focusing your energy and maintaining your levels of motivation will be to specify the exact grade for which you are aiming.

Look After Your Health

Look after your health. This is a fairly obvious piece of advice regarding the effects of tiredness or illness on your overall exam performance, so what follows are some common-sense suggestions which are very familiar though often ignored. They can make a big difference to your motivation, freshness and sharpness.

✔ Eat plenty of fresh fruits, salad and vegetables, take your vitamins and drink plenty of water.

✔ Carry out at the very **least** one vigorous physical activity every week. Make time for it. If you can mix socialising breaks with exercise, so much the better.

✔ Do some simple stretches or exercises if you have been working at a desk for a long period. It will help the flow of blood around your body and into your brain.

✔ Try the following one-minute relaxation technique anywhere and at any time: consciously relax each muscle in your body in turn, beginning with your toes, then work up through the body and finally relax every muscle in your face.

✔ Where possible get regular sleep and meals.

✔ Alcohol affects people in different ways. The occasional drink may help you to relax, but if you feel your study performance is affected by alcohol steer clear of excessive alcohol around the exam. You can compensate afterwards.

SUMMARY

You should now be in a position to...

Make a good start to the day

Find the right time and place to study to ensure you are productive

Access all your important information quickly

Stay motivated

Avoid some of the obstacles which prevented you doing what you intended

Be organised and effective

Make Planning Easy

Planning is the most essential step on the route
to improved performance. Good planning
doesn't depend on a high level of intelligence
and even minor improvements can produce
dramatic effects

Core Principles

Start planning early

Starting to plan early helps you to stay on top of your work and avoid 'fire-fighting'. This is when you fall behind and try chaotically to put out the blaze of work that threatens to engulf you. The quantity of work haunts you even when you are supposed to be relaxing. In other words, you are not in control of the situation, but the deadline and/or pressure is controlling you.

However early you actually planned to start, it is usually your guilty conscience that gets you working seriously. This phenomenon does not usually occur until later into the term and usually goes into overtime as deadlines begin to loom. The aim of any planning system is to convince (or trick) your conscience into bringing forward the point in time at which you begin serious work.

A plan written down in black and white will always help you to start earlier. Plans cause initial alarm because you wonder how the remaining work is going to get done. Therefore, the earlier you plan, the earlier you panic, so the earlier you start work and hence the more in control you are of your workload. Do not forget that you can choose your start date, but the finish date cannot be moved.

Achieve something every day

A fundamental rule is to plan to make a positive contribution to your degree every day. By completing a planned amount of study you will get a warm feeling of accomplishment (or positive achievement). You will also build confidence in your ability to get tasks done. The result will be that you get better at planning and allocating the level of effort to fit your target grade.

There will be occasions where you have somehow to make yourself believe that you achieved what you set out to do for that day so as to maintain that feeling of daily positive achievement, even if it means cutting a corner or two, or cunningly rescheduling some piece of work to another day.

Attain a feeling of positive achievement and you will certainly be more relaxed when doing other things. Levels of stress are cut because you avoid the 'should I..., I want to..., I will later...' attitude. You'll be pleasantly surprised at the positive feeling you get from completing your daily objectives and then unleashing your energy to enjoy the other things you like to do. Skilful planning and scheduling equals stress relief and a consequent reduction in the persistent silent nagging of your conscience. You don't want to be weary; you need to be fresh, alert and in control of the situation.

> Plan a daily task. There is no sense in half wanting to do something, then using up energy worrying about having to do it and ending up doing nothing

Plan for the unexpected using blank days

If you timetable your efforts well in advance and achieve a result every day (excluding the time you have planned away from work), the work will get done. In order to do this, you will need to do something many students never do. That is to

> By achieving something every day you will enjoy your time off all the more

✔ Plan for unexpected situations.

✔ Plan for some tasks to take longer than expected.

✔ Plan for distractions.

> Always plan for the unexpected by inserting blank days into your schedule

Blank (or catch-up) hours or days are used for overruns in your schedule. It's not that you won't keep to your schedule (of course not!), but sometimes something may happen which disrupts you:

✗ watching the television

✗ answering the telephone

✗ oversleeping

✗ overdrinking/illness

✗ hearing of a party at the last minute

✗ somebody calls round to visit and drags you out

✓ someone very sexy calls round to visit

✗ problems back home

✗ bank notifies you about your overdraft

So instead of thinking 'oh *!!*?*' when you finally settle down to work, you should immediately reschedule those actions you cannot complete into the blank hours or days you allowed for in your plan. The aim is systematically to build in blank time to deal with such setbacks. If you have fallen behind because of something unplanned and you do not re-plan, you will fall into a cycle of negative achievement. Then you will get the feeling of always being behind your plan, of not achieving daily objectives, a feeling which can dent your spirits. One day of partial achievement will soon be followed by others, and many things will conspire against you in your efforts to complete your tasks. Therefore, the scheduling of blank hours, days and weeks into your plan is critical. In summary, after any setback – major or minor – quickly re-plan and get into a cycle of positive daily achievement as soon as possible.

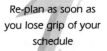

Re-plan as soon as you lose grip of your schedule

Leave enough time to prepare easy-to-learn revision notes

Poor 'planning' will result in poorly 'prepared' revision notes. 'Learning' poorly prepared revision notes will leave you with an unclear understanding of the key concepts. It will also put you at a major disadvantage in terms of the grade you can achieve and the stress you will feel in the weeks and days before the exam. The preparation of 'easy-to-learn' revision notes is one of the most valuable stages of the entire learning process, yet it is also the most rushed (see Figure 5.1).

PLAN   **PREPARE**   **LEARN**

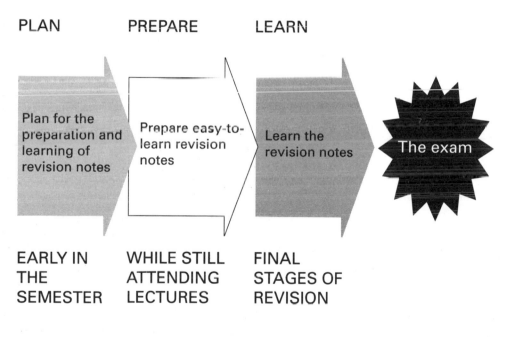

Plan for the preparation and learning of revision notes

Prepare easy-to-learn revision notes

Learn the revision notes

The exam

EARLY IN THE SEMESTER   **WHILE STILL ATTENDING LECTURES**   **FINAL STAGES OF REVISION**

Fig. 5.1
Planning for the preparation of revision notes

We return to the stages of preparing and learning the revision notes in more detail in Chapters 6, 7 and 8, but when *planning* for their preparation consider the two following points:

> Avoid a situation where you wished you had begun preparing your revision notes earlier (and hence left more time to learn them).

> The preparation of revision notes is an activity you will need to begin while you are still attending lectures.

Juggling the preparation of easy-to-learn revision notes (before the course is finished) and your ongoing lecture demands is not easy, but if you can manage it you will sail through the potentially difficult four weeks of final revision and achieve some excellent grades.

If you are doing a subject in which each subsequent lecture helps you to develop your overall understanding from earlier lectures, then you should schedule the preparation of your revision notes towards the end of the semester.

In some subjects, material covered in the later parts of a course can be different to that provided during the early part of the course. In these situations you can begin to prepare easy-to-learn revision notes in parallel to attending the course.

In summary, anticipate when you will have all the information needed to complete the preparation of parts of your revision notes for various subjects and then adjust your plan accordingly (see Figure 5.4 on page 59).

Have a planning system

The key skill in planning and scheduling is being able to write down your plans. It will help to keep your mind free, focused and relaxed when you are either working or doing some other activity. Don't keep your plans in your head as they will eventually clutter up your mind. In general, a good planning system should:

✔ Allow you to add tasks and be easy to change.

✔ Be easy to carry around.

✔ Cope with tasks in the short term and the long term.

✔ Accommodate both your own study style and leisure-time activities.

✔ Convey the actual plan quickly and easily.

If you are using a paper-based planning system try to get into the habit of using a pencil for writing in it. Pens will result in crossings-out as the need to re-plan arises. It then becomes difficult to see what your plans are. The use of pencil allows you to change your schedule quickly, and so you have a clear and well-presented plan. This is important because all the tasks set out in your planning system must feel 'doable'.

The remainder of this chapter details the three key elements of a planning system which are essential during your degree: a diary, a daily timechart and a life checklist (see Figure 5.2).

Diary View the whole year at a glance and experiment with plans leading up to key deadlines

Daily timechart Plan each day in detail

Life checklist Keep a check on non-work-related chores and activities

Fig. 5.2
Key elements of a planning system

Planning Tool 1:
The Diary

Outline-scheduling the semester

There are four steps involved in outline-scheduling the semester. The workload of Johnny 'B' Good is used as an example to explain some of the key points.

➤ **Step 1: Identify the total workload and the length of the semester**

✔ Six exams

✔ Four coursework } 25 weeks before the beginning of exams

✔ One project

➤ **Step 2: Enter the key dates/deadlines for coursework, exams and projects in a diary**

➤ **Step 3: Allocate a bucket of time to the key activities that occur during the semester (see Figure 5.3 below).**

Activity	Activity duration	Total
● Relaxation at the beginning of the semester	2 wks	2
● 4 courseworks	1 wk each	4
● Preparation of easy-to-learn revision notes for the 6 exams	2 wks each	12
● Project work	2 wks	2
● Blank	1 wk	1
● Final stages of revision for the 6 exams	4 wks	4
		25

Fig. 5.3
Allocate buckets of time to key activities

Some points in the above allocation are worth elaborating:

✔ No work is planned during the first two weeks of the semester – it is regarded as a holiday.

✔ One week is allocated as blank between the preparation of easy-to-learn revision notes and the final stages of revision (learning the revision notes) to allow for over-runs. If no overruns occur, then the blank time could be used as an extra holiday. This estimate of blank time is based upon taking major exams twice a year. If your major exams occur only once in the year then at least 10–12 days may be more suitable. Note that all these timings are illustrative only, and that all timings in this and other chapters should be adapted to suit your own circumstances.

Fig. 5.4
Scheduling the activities into the 25 weeks before the exams

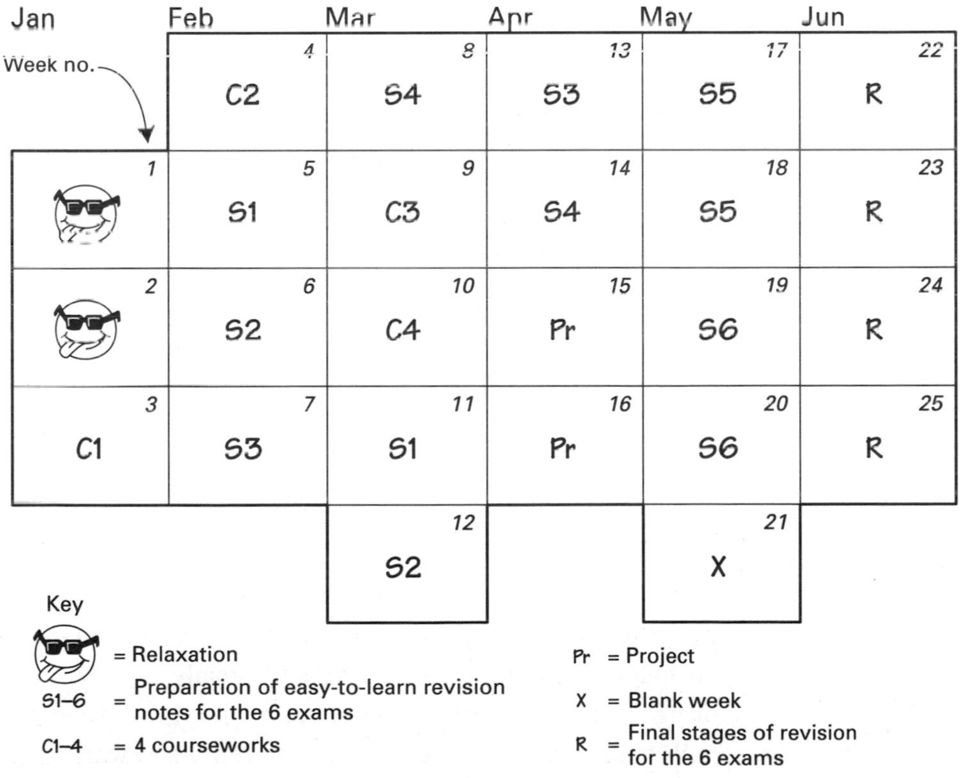

Jan	Feb	Mar	Apr	May	Jun
Week no.	*4* C2	*8* S4	*13* S3	*17* S5	*22* R
1	S1	*5* C3	*9* S4	*14* S5	*18* *23* R
2	S2	*6* C4	*10* Pr	*15* S6	*19* *24* R
3 C1	*7* S3	*11* S1	*16* Pr	*20* S6	*25* R
		12 S2		*21* X	

Key

= Relaxation

S1–6 = Preparation of easy-to-learn revision notes for the 6 exams

C1–4 = 4 courseworks

Pr = Project

X = Blank week

R = Final stages of revision for the 6 exams

➤ **Step 4: Schedule the activities**

Having allocated a bucket of time to each activity, the next step is to schedule the activities into a diary (see Figure 5.4 on page 59). It takes less than five minutes to plan the semester in this way, and it will spur you on to take control of your work and begin a cycle of positive achievement.

How many actual study days are there in a week?

When outline-scheduling the semester, you need to know the number of days you can expect to work in a week so that your plans are realistic (see Figure 5.5). Calculate the number of **study days** in a week by *subtracting* the number of days you will reasonably need for:

✔ Doing no work, going away for the weekend, going home, relaxing etc.

✔ Catching up on things which you had underestimated in your plan or which you didn't expect.

Number of days in a week	*7*
Subtract	
No. of days off in a week	*1.5*
Catch-up days	*0.5*
Number of study days left in a week	*5*

Fig. 5.5
Calculating the
number of study
days in a week

The planning approach described in this section should encourage you on to get going early. As with running a race, it is helpful to make a good start, set a steady rhythm, and leave enough room for the (inevitable) sprint finish. Next we shall consider a technique for planning your daily work.

Planning Tool 2:
The Daily Planner

Study in short bursts to maintain a high level of concentration

Before devising the layout of your daily planner, you need to decide upon the pattern of time in which you work most effectively. Let us begin by making two general observations regarding levels of concentration in two familiar study situations.

In a lecture, you may find that you concentrate most clearly for the first ten minutes (when you are fresh) and the last ten minutes (when you know the lecture is coming to an end). In an exam, one of the reasons you can do a lot of work in a very short time is because you have the clear aim of answering a question as 'fully' as you can within a very specific time limit. Combine these two observations in your study sessions (as described below in the form of two workable principles) and you will be able to concentrate the whole time and re-create a working intensity often reserved for the exams:

1 Plan to work in short bursts of energy spaced with frequently planned breaks.

2 Every short burst should be fixed in length and contain a set study task.

There are times when we all prefer to work for a longer period and it can sometimes take a while to develop the momentum required to complete a task. Nevertheless, you will be surprised at the effect of using shorter bursts of energy. With a little practice it is possible to **train** the mind to work in shorter bursts, so that you are able to hit 'full flow' more quickly. You will also increase your working stamina and therefore be able to work more productively throughout the day.

Developing a time pattern for effective study

As an example, you may find it useful to split *every* hour of revision into two study sessions of 25 and 20 minutes. A five-minute break should be taken between the two study sessions, with a ten-minute break at the end. This can more simply be described as the 25-(5)-20-(10) one-hour time period for study, where the number in brackets denotes the period of relaxation (see Figure 5.6). The advantages of the 25-(5)-20-(10) one-hour time pattern for study are as follows:

✔ The breaks allow for overruns in the planned revision.

✔ The one-hour study session begins with a longer 25-minute session and ends with the shorter 20-minute session because it is more comforting to get the longer session out of the way first.

✔ When you have to cope with study in short bursts, the next break is never that far away.

✔ Defined study sessions will encourage you to schedule your work more effectively.

✔ Sessions that begin and end on the hour are easier to plan and psyche yourself up for.

✔ It is possible to fit in two hard study sessions in an hour, or four hard study sessions in two hours, and so on.

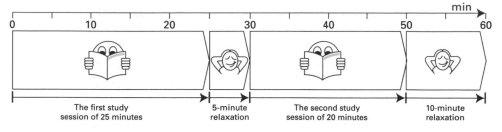

The first study session of 25 minutes — 5-minute relaxation — The second study session of 20 minutes — 10-minute relaxation

You may choose to vary your study pattern depending on the level of concentration demanded by the study task (see Figure 5.7). Try to mark out at least one-quarter of every hour of study as relaxation. In addition, try to ensure that your study patterns are multiples of 30 minutes so that it is easy to schedule into a daily planner. Consider the following alternatives to the 25-(5)-20-(10) study pattern:

Fig. 5.6
The 25-(5)-20-(10) one-hour time pattern for study

Explore different time patterns of study for different study tasks

- ✓ Try a 45-(15) if you need a lot of relaxation between study sessions.

- ✓ Try a 30-(30) if you often underestimate how long it takes you to complete a task.

- ✓ Try a 50-(10) if you prefer longer revision sessions.

- ✓ Try a 60-(30) if you prefer to work a full hour before relaxation.

- ✓ Try a 90-(30) for a less intense two-hour study session.

More intense study

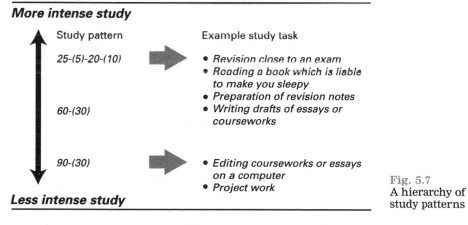

Study pattern	Example study task
25-(5)-20-(10)	• Revision close to an exam • Reading a book which is liable to make you sleepy • Preparation of revision notes
60-(30)	• Writing drafts of essays or courseworks
90-(30)	• Editing courseworks or essays on a computer • Project work

Less intense study

Fig. 5.7
A hierarchy of study patterns

Designing your personalised daily planner

Don't neglect to check your progress on your outline schedule of the semester and update your daily objectives

Having decided upon your pattern of study, you will need to draw it up in the form of your own personalised daily planner. Figure 5.8 shows how a day is carved up using the 25-(5)-20-(10) time pattern for study. A master schedule for seven days should be made to fill a single sheet of A4. Produce copies to cover the weeks until the next set of exams. Use symbols (see Figure 5.9) as well as text to complete the daily planner, so that you can quickly review the plans.

Fill in your daily planner in cycles of about two weeks in length. For the last four weeks before the exam, fill in the daily planner for all four of those weeks.

	Sun	Mon	Tue	Wed	Thu	Fri	Sat
8.00–8.25							
8.30–8.50							
9.00–9.25							
9.00–9.50							
10.00–10.25							
10.30–10.50							

Fig. 5.8
A daily planner based on the 25-(5)-20-(10) time pattern for study

Activity	Symbol	Activity	Symbol
Sleep		Getting ready	
Study		Going out	
Relaxation		Listening to music	
Meal		Playing sport	
Travelling	 RETURN	Enjoy	

The daily planner: An example

Fig. 5.9
Symbols to aid
planning

Now let us consider how Johnny 'B' Good transformed his minimum objective for Monday (to complete nine questions of an exam and attend a one-hour lecture) into a detailed plan. He allowed almost half an hour per exam question and left one hour as blank to allow for overruns (see Figure 5.10). Johnny scheduled the nine exam questions in three sessions:

✔ Session 1   2 hrs

✔ Session 2   1.5 hrs

✔ Session 3   1 hr

The same principles that apply to scheduling a group of study sessions apply to scheduling an hour of study. Aim to begin with a longer session when you are fresh so that you can make a good start. Take longer breaks between the later sessions to allow for tiredness and overruns.

	Sun	Mon	Tue	Wed	Thu	Fri	Sat
8.00–8.25							
8.25–8.50		RETURN					
9.00–9.25		Lecture					
9.30–9.50		Lecture					
10.00–10.25							
10.30–10.50		RETURN					
11.00–11.25		Question 1					
11.30–11.50		Question 2	A two-hour				
12.00–12.25		Question 3	session				
12.30–12.50		Question 4					
1.00–1.25							
1.30–1.50							
2.00–2.25		Question 5					
2.30–2.50		Question 6	A one-and-a-half				
3.00–3.25		Question 7	hour session				
3.30–3.50							
4.00–4.25		Question 8	A one-hour				
4.30–4.50		Question 9	session				
5.00–5.25		Blank					
5.30–5.50		Blank					
6.00–6.25							
6.30–6.50							
7.00–7.25							
7.30–7.50							
8.00–8.25							
8.30–8.50							
9.00–9.25							
9.30–9.50							
10.00–10.25							
10.30–10.50							
11.00–11.25							
11.30–11.50							

Fig. 5.10
Filling in the
daily planner

How many productive study hours are there in a day?

Having filled in the tasks on your daily planner, you will quickly realise just how few hours there are in a day to actually study. Excluding the days before a major coursework deadline or exam, I believe there are at least four but not more than six hours of productive study time in a day.

Always remember that it is not the number of hours worked that counts. You must focus on completing the tasks you planned for that day regardless of whether they last five minutes or five hours. The upshot of this approach is that you will have to work extremely hard to complete your tasks for that day, or work into the relaxation time, or reschedule the remainder of the tasks!

Do not **plan** more than 4–6 study hours in a day

It is excellent practice to schedule at least one activity every day that is non-work-related. This should act as a strong incentive for you to complete the quantity of study you had planned.

Focus on the completion of tasks and not on how much time you spend working

Planning Tool 3:
Life Checklists

It is important to maintain the feeling of daily positive achievement in all aspects of degree life. Organising your study tasks is one thing, but you are more than likely to be doing a multitude of other things at the same time. To get on with your work, you must make sure that you have a clear head, so all those irritating little things that need doing must get done. These activities should be clearly written down in lists; they generally consist of telephoning, writing,

Keep on top of the things to do outside your work

buying, organising, visiting, and so on. Divide these activities into two lists which:

✔ Must be done **NOW** (see Figure 5.11).

✔ Can be done **LATER** (see Figure 5.12).

Fig 5.11
Example of life
checklist: Now

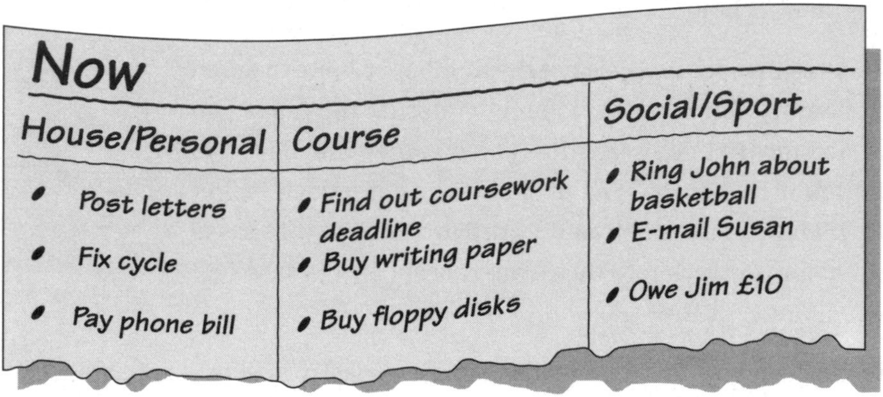

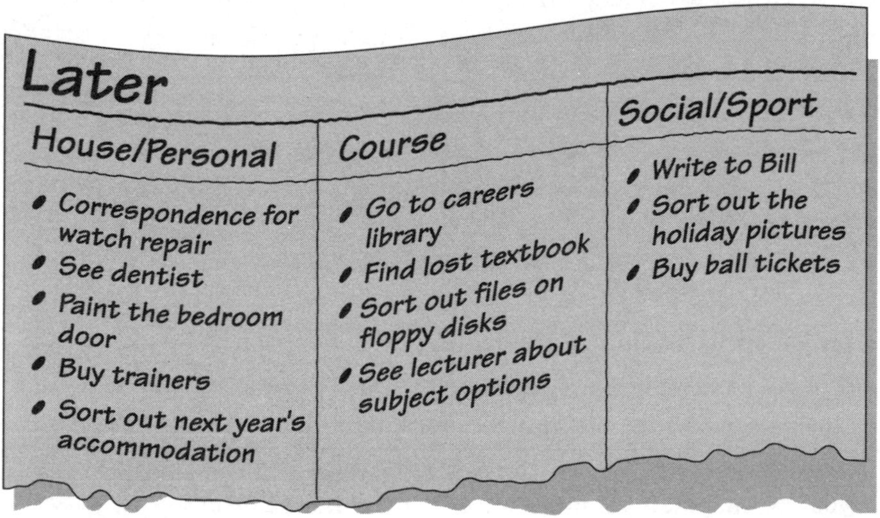

Now

House/Personal	Course	Social/Sport
• Post letters	• Find out coursework deadline	• Ring John about basketball
• Fix cycle	• Buy writing paper	• E-mail Susan
• Pay phone bill	• Buy floppy disks	• Owe Jim £10

Later

House/Personal	Course	Social/Sport
• Correspondence for watch repair	• Go to careers library	• Write to Bill
• See dentist	• Find lost textbook	• Sort out the holiday pictures
• Paint the bedroom door	• Sort out files on floppy disks	• Buy ball tickets
• Buy trainers	• See lecturer about subject options	
• Sort out next year's accommodation		

Fig. 5.12
Example of life
checklist: Later

The 'later' list contains activities which are outside your immediate priorities. Some of these things may subsequently become urgent, and some of them you're not likely ever to do, but at least having them written down will be enough to ease your conscience.

Each of these two lists can be further divided into any number of categories, e.g. house, course, social, etc. These lists can easily be arranged on large post-it notes and applied to the inside cover of your pocket diary (see Figure 5.13).

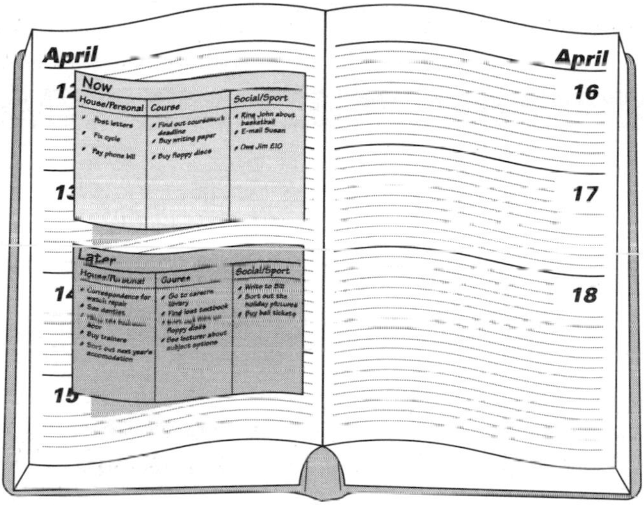

Fig. 5.13
Possible arrangements of post-it notes in a diary

Life checklists are beneficial because they give you an instant visual reminder of the things you need to get done. If you are planning a trip to town, they help you avoid getting home only to realise that something has been forgotten. Order the activities on a post-it note and tick them off as you go along (see Figure 5.14 on page 70). However simple the activity is, it always feels good to have completed a task and be in a position to cross it off your list.

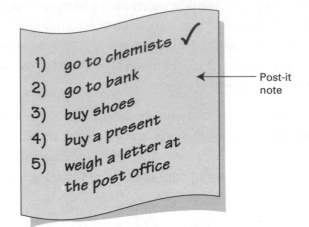

Post-it
note

Fig. 5.14
Ordering activities
on a trip to town

SUMMARY

This chapter detailed a practical approach to planning which will help you to enjoy other things in your degree life. The approach advocates studying with an uncluttered mind, improving concentration and making a positive contribution every day.

Pick up supplies that help you to enjoy the planning experience

Finally, bear in mind that we have detailed only one example of a planning system. Many other variations based on the same key principles will be just as good. Visit an office supplies store and you will find a wide range of planning tools. Try an **electronic** personal organiser if you are unsuited to a paper-based system.

You will now be in a position to...

Write a clear plan up to the next set of exams

Start early

Achieve something every day

Plan for the unexpected using catch-up days

Schedule time to prepare easy-to-learn revision notes

Calculate the number of productive study days in a week

Develop your own time pattern for effective study

Study in short bursts and enjoy frequent breaks

Fill in a daily planner

Plan non-work-related activities

Work less, learn more and relax more

Planning Courseworks and Exam Reviews

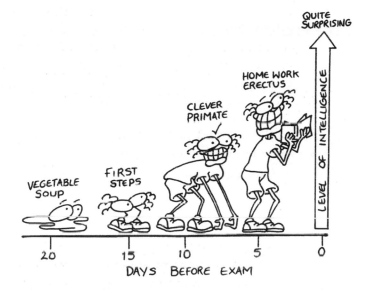

Special planning and review skills are essential to ensure that you reach your peak of knowledge on the day you submit a coursework or take an exam

Planning Courseworks

Share information and start early

Courseworks can be demanding on your time, but it is possible to pick up high marks to ease the pressure on your examination performance. Consider the following points to improve your effectiveness in courseworks:

✔ A coursework task is often exactly the same for everyone in the class; there is an obvious opportunity to share information and improve your grade. The help and support of your friends will be invaluable during the preparation of courseworks.

✔ It is important to understand the difficult parts of a coursework as early as possible. You will need time to get the information you need (from lecturers, friends, libraries) to tackle these difficulties.

✔ If you spend enough time on the courseworks, and therefore if your scheduling is good, you are likely to be good at courseworks.

Teamwork is discussed in more detail in Chapter 11

✔ If you begin work on the coursework early you will be in a very strong position to trade your ideas and knowledge on how you tackled the coursework with other people in your class. If you trust your classmates, you should not feel uncomfortable in lending them a copy of your coursework. They can give you useful comments and won't just steal the 'best bits'. Equally, they will feel comfortable in lending you their coursework. You can then use it to appraise the strengths and weaknesses of your own work.

Alternatively, suppose you are less enthusiastic about the coursework and you are not too worried about getting a top grade. Try to fall into the slipstream of someone who is prepared to break into all the new ground and then share that information with you.

In the event of an emergency (you have prepared nothing on a coursework that must be handed in tomorrow), you will no doubt be calling in a few favours or have to beg to see an already completed coursework from a friend. If you find yourself in this position, beg to see completed courseworks from at least two friends, and be sure to add something distinctive from your own thoughts!

Setting deadlines for courseworks

To ensure that you leave enough time to prepare easy-to-learn revision notes, you must become an expert at setting and achieving deadlines on your courseworks. There are two types of coursework deadline:

✓ **Internal deadlines:** These are deadlines that you set for yourself to ensure you leave sufficient time to complete the other study activities.

✓ **External deadlines:** These are the deadlines the lecturer sets for you.

Keeping to internal deadlines is very important because you are able to:

✓ Carry out the next activity in your schedule with the full amount of time allocated to it.

✓ Actually rest when you had planned (the feeling that you have to catch up on a task that has got out of hand will contribute to a feeling of negative achievement).

✓ Keep to your schedule to stay fresh and motivated.

Let's suppose you planned to do something in three days, but owing to unforeseen circumstances the task was a little more complicated than you anticipated and you only have one day left. For the above reasons, it is important that you find a way to fit a shortcut version of the outstanding work within your existing internal deadline. For example, this might entail cutting back on some of the intended background reading. Or, as suggested in Chapter 5, you could reschedule part of the activity into the blank time you allowed for overruns.

Be ruthless and stick to your internal deadlines, otherwise you may be taking time away from other essential activities or, worse, robbing yourself of vital rest

Two further closely related points are worth taking into account when planning your coursework. Always set the internal deadline to finish at least two or three days in advance of the external deadline (set by the lecturer). And always schedule in at least one special day to cope with any last-minute ideas or improvements you may have. It is during these one or two days before the external deadline that:

✔ The most fervent discussions about the content of the courseworks will take place with your classmates.

✔ The lecturers are tempted to drop the most generous hints.

✔ The hardest work is put in by most of the people in the class. As a result the whole class will undergo a steep learning curve. So be ready to take advantage of this knowledge and make as many last-minute adjustments as necessary.

Figure 6.1 provides an example of how two courseworks could be scheduled using the principles outlined above. The internal deadlines are planned well in advance of the external deadlines. Blank days are allocated just after the internal deadline to allow for an overrun. A special day is

allocated to each coursework before every external deadline
to allow for any final adjustments. Immovable rest days are
allocated to both Sundays to do some other activity.

Fig. 6.1
Planning two
courseworks

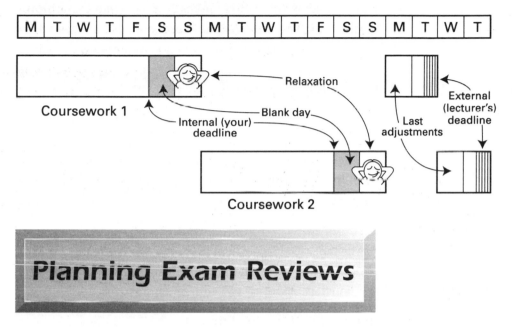

Planning Exam Reviews

A pattern of review for long-term memory

You may have come across a pattern of review which has
been scientifically proven to improve long-term memory
(described as the 'conventional' approach in this chapter). It
recommends that after the first reading the material should
be read for about ten minutes at the following intervals:

✔ 5 minutes

✔ 1 hour

✔ 1 day

✔ 1 week

✔ 1 month, etc.

It is fair to say that students do not actually follow this pattern of revision. Even the most committed would find it hard to follow such a regime. The approach is difficult to plan and implement, and this makes it impossible to maintain motivation. The conventional approach also suggests that you cannot do the bulk of the revision in the weeks and days before an exam. This is not really true, as any student who has ever taken an exam at university will already know.

The conventional approach will work if you want to commit such information to your long-term memory; however, your aim is **not** to train your memory to learn for some possible event in the future but to perform in an exam on a highly specific date.

On top of this, there is simply not enough time to commit all of the massive amounts of information given on a degree course to long-term memory. This must mean you have to develop the capabilities of your short-term memory.

In summary, it is your ability to assimilate information in a short space of time as well as your knowledge of the subject that is examined. Therefore, if you want to do better in exams, you will have to develop a pattern of review which is designed to develop your short-term recall. This in turn ensures that you will be able to peak on the day of the exam.

A pattern of review for short-term memory

The key principles underlying the preferred pattern of review in this book are that as the exam approaches, the reviews become more frequent. You are able to fit in more reviews as the exam approaches because:

Reviews should take place more frequently and take less time as the exam approaches

✔ Every review takes less time as you become more familiar with the material.

✓ You will certainly have a high level of motivation (or sense of urgency!).

For a 25-week semester the following pattern of review is suggested, with the approximate time for review in brackets. Again, note that the number of reviews and the length of the reviews are illustrative only and that they should be adapted to suit your own requirements.

Stage 1: Preparation of easy-to-learn revision notes

➤ **4–21 weeks before the exam (1–2 weeks per subject).**

- Do not try to memorise the material during this first review. Focus on developing a sound understanding of the topic area which is reflected in revision notes that are easy to learn. This will also enable you to review your notes more quickly as the exam approaches.

  Allow approximately 1–2 weeks per subject to prepare easy-to-learn revision notes

- It is preferable (discretely!) to prepare as many of your easy-to-learn revision notes as possible during the Christmas and Easter vacations. This will ensure that it is a lot easier to fit in the balance of the work around your other study activities during term time.
- An example of scheduling the preparation of easy-to-learn revision notes is illustrated in Figures 5.3 and 5.4 in Chapter 5 (see pages 58–9).
- Refer to Chapters 7 and 8 to discover how to produce easy-to-learn revision notes.

Stage 2: Learning the revision notes

➤ **4 weeks before the exam (1 to 2 days per subject).**

- The countdown through the final stages of review begins here.
- This will be your first attempt to learn the revision notes.

➤ **14 days before the exam (half a day per subject)**

➤ **7 days before the exam (half a day per subject)**

➤ **4 days before the exam (half a day per subject)**

➤ **2 days before the exam (half a day per subject)**

➤ **Multiple reviews in 24 hours before the exam (2 hours per subject)**

- You are now in a position rapidly to review all the essential points two to three times in these 24 hours before the exam. This is an essential skill especially if your exams are very close together. Techniques for rapid review are discussed in Chapter 10.

If you follow the above pattern of review, the change in the level of your learning should be represented by a snake-like curve (see Figures 6.2 and 6.3). In the moments just before the exam you should be bursting with knowledge. The exam itself will be a form of cleansing in which you set free from your mind all the knowledge related to that subject. After the exam, reload your mind with knowledge using your easy-to-learn revision notes in readiness for the next exam.

Fig. 6.2
The pattern of review for short-term memory showing the resultant change in level of knowledge prior to the exam

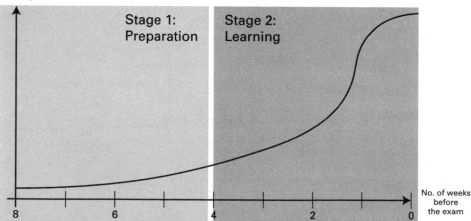

Level of knowledge in subject

Stage 1: Preparation

Stage 2: Learning

No. of weeks before the exam

8   6   4   2   0

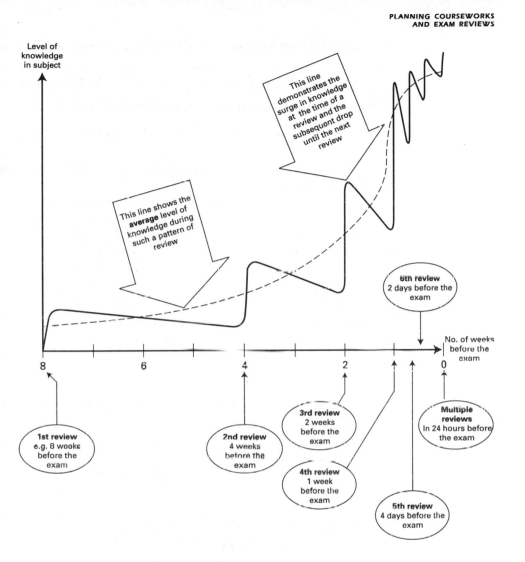

Level of
knowledge
in subject

This line
demonstrates the
surge in knowledge
at the time of a
review and the
subsequent drop
until the next
review

This line shows the
average level of
knowledge during
such a pattern of
review

6th review
2 days before the
exam

No. of weeks
before the
exam

8   6   4   2   0

1st review
e.g. 8 weeks
before the
exam

2nd review
4 weeks
before the
exam

3rd review
2 weeks
before the
exam

4th review
1 week
before the
exam

5th review
4 days before the
exam

Multiple
reviews
In 24 hours before
the exam

Overall, the conventional approach to review requires too much effort too far away from the exam, and because it is an approach focused on learning for the long term, you don't peak for the exam. The result is wasted effort.

The approach in this book encourages you to review more vigorously as you get closer to the exam date so that you peak at the time of the exam. And because you are close to the exam you have the motivation actually to do it.

Fig. 6.3
The pattern of
review for short-
term memory
showing the
change in level of
knowledge after
each review

The aim is to prepare only for that specific one-off event – your examinations. Starting early with the preparation of a good set of easy-to-learn revision notes and well-planned frequent reviews as the exam approaches will ensure that your short-term memory will be utilised to the fullest. You'll be staggered at just how much you can pump into your memory.

It may be argued that such an approach puts you under extra pressure closer to the exam. But I believe that pressure around examination time is an inevitable fact of college/university life. And the best thing you can do to alleviate this pressure is to have written down in your plan exactly the number of reviews you have left, and have the confidence to know you can learn everything in your revision notes from these remaining reviews. Until you have been through a high-pressure learning situation, you would never have believed just how much can be learned.

Of course there would be difficulties if you were to fall ill. But so close to an exam your body will somehow hold off the illness because it knows it needs to perform; the pressure will lead your body to raise its performance. If you have begun your set of reviews sufficiently early, and a planned review gets missed through emergency or illness, then you can easily make up ground on the next review.

You should also be able to cope if a review gets missed very close to the exam because you will have already completed a good number of reviews and your knowledge in that subject will be at a high level. Overall, the early start, the number of reviews and the timing of the reviews will give you a certain level of built-in safety that will enable you to cope with the unexpected.

SUMMARY

Planning courseworks: You will now be in a position to...

Start early

Set deadlines that do not impact on subsequent study activities

Share and trade information with others

Plan time for last-minute adjustments

Submit a coursework to a high standard and minimise effort

Planning exam reviews: You will now be in a position to...

Allow time to prepare easy-to-learn revision notes

Plan more frequent but shorter reviews as the exam approaches

Develop your short-term memory recall for a specific event

Cope with a missed review

Peak on the day of the exam

Concurrent Revision

Learning is a two-stage process. This chapter considers how information should be prepared to avoid wasted effort before it is learned. Answers to past exam papers, background reading, lecture notes and your extended understanding of the subject should be considered concurrently, not sequentially. The aim is to prepare a single set of easy-to-learn revision notes that contains all the information you need for the exam

Prepare for Exams Using Concurrent Revision

Introduction

Concurrent revision
is a key skill that will
avoid duplication of
effort and help you
to learn faster

Information used in the exam will be assimilated from four key sources:

1 Lecture notes.

2 Questions and answers to past exam papers.

3 Background reading.

4 Your own extended understanding of the subject.

Let's imagine these four sources of information are considered sequentially (i.e. one after the other). Similar information will be presented to the mind in four slightly different ways. This has the potential to cause confusion, especially if there is a lot of information to be learned. The result will be an answer in the examination that is lacking both in depth and clarity.

If you rewrite lecture notes, make further notes on background reading, prepare separate answers for the exam paper and then add your own thoughts all **at different times**, you are likely to have included material in these sets of notes that is not required for the exam. This results in more subject material to learn and makes it less likely that you will include in the exam what is actually relevant.

The aim of concurrent revision is to combine the three written sets of information (see 1, 2 and 3 above) into a consistent, focused and relevant set of revision notes, and then immediately to add the fourth set of information from your own extended understanding of the subject. To pre-pare four sets of revision notes on the same subject at different times is a complete waste of time. Clearly, it would be much more sensible to create one set of easy-to-learn revision notes by analysing these four sources concurrently (at the same time). See Figure 7.1 for a summary of the concurrent revision approach.

As a result of having recently reviewed the relevant sources and recorded this detailed understanding, you will have produced a set of revision notes that will be easy to learn, consistent and show an in-depth understanding of the topic area. At the final stages of revision, it is psychologically reassuring to know that you have reduced the lecture notes, background reading and exam questions to a **single** well-prepared set of revision notes, which should therefore contain everything you need to know in the exam.

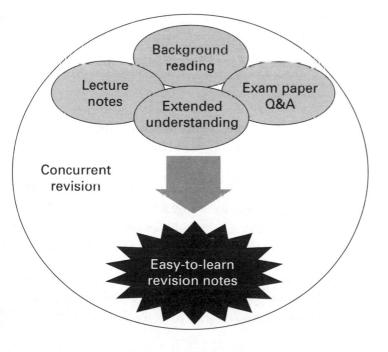

Fig. 7.1
Concurrent
revision

How to apply concurrent revision

The key steps of the concurrent revision approach are described as follows:

1 Cluster or group similar questions from past exam papers into topics. Let us assume that five topics have been identified.

2 Identify the lecture material which corresponds to each of these five topics.

3 Identify in advance the areas of background reading which are relevant to these five topics.

4 Allocate a bucket of time for this first review in which the easy-to-learn revision notes are prepared. Let us suggest that you allow two weeks to complete this first review in which there are ten actual study days (see Figures 5.4 and 5.5 on pages 59–60). Therefore two days are available to tackle each of the five topics. This is not a lot of time, especially if you are attending lectures at the same time. Steps 1 to 4 are summarised in Table 7.1.

5 Do the preparatory reading required to write the easy-to-learn revision notes:

✔ Read the cluster of exam questions which correspond to that one specific topic only.

✔ Read the relevant lecture notes in detail.

✔ Read the relevant background material to deepen your understanding of the subject and to clarify difficulties.

6 Write the easy-to-learn revision notes in the form of detailed answers to the cluster of similar exam questions you had earlier identified for each topic area. The

answers are taken from the lecture notes and the background reading while it is all fresh in your mind. At this point you should force yourself to make early and tough decisions about what you think you need to know in the exams.

7 Having just prepared a first draft of the revision notes, now is the perfect time to add your own extended understanding of the subject.

Table. 7.1
Concurrent
revision, steps
1 to 4

Topic numbers	Lecture numbers	Question no. (from last year's exam paper)	Question no. (from penultimate year's exam paper)	Background reading	Time allocated
1	1, 2, 3	1a, b	1a, b	Book A, pp.0–20	2 days
2	4, 5	2a, b	2a	Article B, C, D	2 days
3	6, 7	3a, b	2b, 3a, 3b	Article E, F	2 days
4	8, 9	4a, b	4a, b	Book G, pp.60–100	2 days
5	10	5a, b	5a, b	Book H, pp.0–50	2 days
Total					10 days

Past Papers

Introduction

As stated in Chapter 3, exam papers should be obtained as soon as possible in the term. Not only does this get the shock out of the way early on, it also provides relevance to the lecture material and, more importantly, enables you to develop a strategy for tackling the exam paper.

A past paper provides a reasonable indication of what you can expect in future papers. The key is to use past papers to provide a focal point for your revision notes, but to have the flexibility to tackle questions in the event of a significantly different exam paper. Therefore, concentrating your whole revision effort solely on past exam papers is not recommended. The development of your knowledge will be restricted and there is a higher risk you will put in the exam paper what you hope the examiner is asking rather than what the examiner actually wants.

It is always useful to tackle some past papers under timed exam conditions, but this should generally be carried out during the last stages of your revision effort. As suggested earlier in this chapter, your effort should be directed at creating a single set of revision notes that is sufficiently thorough to cover all likely exam questions. This approach will put you in a much stronger position for the actual exam. It will also increase your confidence when you successfully complete whole past papers as the exam date approaches.

The lecturer

In judging the level of flexibility you require in your revision notes (that is, the ability to cope with different questions) you need to find out what type of lecturer is marking your paper. Listen carefully to what is said during the lectures, ask directly, look for patterns across past papers, or talk to students from previous years. Lecturers generally fall into two categories:

✔ Category A lecturers like to stray from the syllabus and explore your wider appreciation of the subject. These lecturers can be described as high risk and therefore you should explore the subject syllabus in more detail and make sure your revision notes are more 'flexible'.

✓ Category B lecturers are happier to keep well within the lecture material provided in the class and will repeat the same pattern of exam questions used in all the previous years. These lecturers are lower risk and their exam papers provide generous scope for question spotting.

Question spotting

Not much needs to be said about question spotting. Students are required to learn a lot of material in a very short time, particularly around exam time. Therefore it is not surprising that students have a highly developed instinct to spot questions.

Question spotting is a valuable technique for saving time

If you like taking a risk, question spotting is a wonderful way of cutting back on the quantity of revision you have to carry out. This is irresistible for some, if not all, students. For example, if the exam paper gives you a choice of three from five questions, you could avoid 20 per cent of your revision by revising only four of the five questions and still allow yourself a margin of safety. If you strongly suspect that a question from a specific topic will or will not appear in the exam, then that provides a further opportunity to target your effort.

Tips from lecturers

Always talk to your lecturers close to the exams; they will have just set the exam questions and they might not be able to avoid giving you a useful tip (or two) in the process. Perhaps they will mention parts of the lecture material you can ignore or give an indication as to which questions are very likely to appear in the exam. Always emphasise how much more demanding the workload of their subject is over other lecturers to help them to talk. Here are three suggested approaches for speaking to your lecturer about the exam paper:

✔ Arrange a private visit in the week before the exam. Lecturers should make themselves available for you to ask questions at this time.

✔ Attend the special revision class in which lecturers go through past papers and give you a chance to ask questions.

✔ Be prepared with questions at the end of the last scheduled lecture before the exam.

Background Reading

Integrating background reading into your revision notes

Background reading is an essential part of preparing your revision notes, especially where the lecture notes are sparse. It will help you to understand, link and further explore information contained in your lecture notes.

How you incorporate the knowledge gained from the background reading into an exam answer deserves special attention. Students often do the background reading that helps their immediate understanding of the subject, but fail to integrate these key points into their revision notes. Unless you are able to recall the salient points of that background reading while you are in the examination, you are not making the best use of the background reading you have done.

On the other hand, be careful not to record too much of the background reading in your revision notes. It might leave you too much to learn. Therefore, read the lecture notes and past exam papers in combination with the background reading to help you to stay focused on the material you need to read.

Scanning techniques and imposing a time limit on your background reading

Background reading can be very time consuming; you should choose carefully what you need to read for the exam, in what detail you need to read it, and the time you allow yourself to read it. Scanning techniques and setting a time limit will help you to avoid reading too much of the book and stop you from reading an interesting but irrelevant section.

It's crucial that you learn to get from your background reading only what you need and in the time you have available

Never just pick up a book and begin reading it from page one. Scan through the contents and then the main body of a book in a couple of minutes to see which sections are the most relevant. Then read the introductory and closing lines of the chapters or paragraphs to verify the book's relevance to your area of study before you read that section in detail.

Scanning will provide you with an insight into the usefulness of the information in the book

Do not be scared to put a time limit on the amount of time you have to read an article, chapter or book. Such time limits will encourage you to scan the book at high speed. The result will be increased reading efficiency as you are forced to read more material in less time.

Extend Your Understanding of the Subject

Breathe life into your thinking by being in touch with the outside world. The process of learning will also become a lot more interesting

Examiners are always highly impressed by the inclusion of relevant material from outside the standard lecture notes. Relate your work to the things going on around you to encourage creative, lateral and innovative thinking. You can look for inspiration from cinema, television documentaries, newspapers, journals, exhibitions, museums, fieldwork, industrial visits, relatives, working people or friends in different subject areas. Study groups are also a superb way to quickly extend your understanding of a subject. Sharing information in this way allows you to discuss wild thoughts and build upon the knowledge and experience gained by others, but more importantly, chatting about the subject can strengthen your confidence in it.

The types of study activity where there is a more involved interaction with the outside world will help you to develop additional key points for inclusion in the exam paper. Having pushed the limits of your understanding, do not forget to add these original thoughts to your revision notes so that your extended understanding of the subject will be properly reflected in your exam answer.

SUMMARY

You should now be in a position to...

Prepare easy-to-learn revision notes having just read the lecture notes, background material, past exam papers and added your own extended understanding of the subject. The knowledge is fresh in your mind and it is easier to create a detailed set of revision notes which are consistent, relevant and focused on potential exam papers

Prepare Easy-to-Learn Revision Notes Using Spider-Diagrams

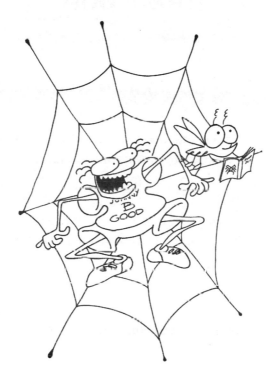

Preparing spider-diagrams is an essential technique for organising and presenting information for super-fast mental digestion. Information is linked and prioritised using fewer words and more pictures

Introduction

Spiders applied to the preparation of revision notes

This chapter describes an approach to writing easy-to-learn revision notes using spider-diagrams. The spider or spider's web is a very useful metaphor when applied to note-taking. For example, a spider has a main body with divisions on which legs are attached, while a spider's web is composed of threads and lines in a web-like arrangement.

The spider analogy is used to describe what is different about the method of note-taking in this chapter. But the aim of this chapter is for you to develop a style of note-taking which ensures your revision notes are as easy to learn as possible.

What is a spider-diagram?

A spider-diagram is a diagrammatic association of words, phrases, lines, arrows and pictures. Spider-diagrams are a fantastic way to structure and prioritise ideas and show the relationship between them.

Revision notes in the form of a spider-diagram will help you to prepare the information in a way that is quickly and easily digested by your mind during the final stages of revision. This will have the effect of significantly improving your learning speed and provide a leap in your learning capacity.

Apply your style of note-taking to different learning situations

Revision notes are a very special way of presenting information; they are a form of shorthand that is very individual to you, because only you will have to use them. Therefore, when you have found a style of note-taking that is able to quickly transfer knowledge, then do not ignore its adaptability to other different learning situations. It could be applied equally well to the preparation of courseworks, summarising of articles and books, organisation of your thoughts, making quickfire notes in a meeting with a supervisor, development of ideas, preparation for interviews, etc.

Spider-Diagrams:
Nine Core Principles

The following section describes nine core principles which you should apply to your spider-diagram to make your revision notes as easy to learn as possible.

1 Customise your spider-diagrams: Your way is the best way

What level of detail should you include in your spider-diagrams and what style of spider-diagram should you use? There is neither a completely right way or a completely wrong way. There are many considerations when preparing a spider-diagram. It depends on the purpose of your spider-diagrams and what style suits you (see Figures 8.7 to 8.10 on pages 108–10).

For example, you are most likely to choose a very different style of spider-diagram depending on the:

✔ Subject type.

✔ Complexity of the exam question. Certain styles of note-taking are better suited to a complex exam question that requires you to apply information in a very high level of detail.

✔ Extent to which you prefer to replace sentences written in straight lines with keywords, links and pictures.

✔ Time you have available to prepare it, the level of legibility you require to read it, and how often you need to review it. The result could either be a very beautiful or a very scruffy spider-diagram.

2 Use pictures to exercise more of your brain

Wherever possible, add a picture to your revision notes. It doesn't have to be a masterpiece; remember, only you will need to see it and use it. Do not deliberate when creating a picture; your aim is to produce a freehand picture very quickly. To heighten the effect that the picture will have on your mind, use colour, exaggerate shapes and generally make it as wild and unusual as possible.

Pictures and sketches are a very powerful aid to memory because you are exercising more of the brain (especially the right-hand side) during the preparation, absorption and testing of your revision notes. If you are able to combine pictures successfully with your words you will create a distinctive and vivid image which is much more easily remembered. In summary, a picture or a sketch will help you to:

✔ Improve your understanding of the key points.

✔ Absorb the key points more quickly.

✔ Add much-needed energy and vitality to your revision notes.

3 Link your thoughts because your mind works that way

It is worth remembering that writing in straight lines and sentences is the way in which we communicate with each other to avoid misunderstanding. But when you are creating a set of revision notes, you are creating patterns of ideas and information which only you need to understand. This opens the way for a radically different method of communication.

A link or diagrammatic association is a way of capturing information on a blank piece of paper that will allow you to break free from convention and express ideas, thoughts and information in a way which only you need to find comfortable. The presentation of information using links and associations will ensure that you improve your ability to learn, because you are writing revision notes in a way in which a mind actually works.

This is very easy to prove, if you were required to explain to your friends your routine for making it into the lecture room in the morning. It would be something like: switch off alarm, get out of bed, go to toilet, brush teeth, have shower, get dressed, have breakfast, leave home and, finally, take the bus to college/university. You can *remember* a story such as this perfectly because your mind works through information that was linked in this instance by a logical sequence of events.

Link information in any way that you think will help you to remember it

When you are preparing your revision notes it will not matter how the information is linked. The link may be logical but it could also be unusual or even absurd. As long as you are able to trick your mind into thinking that there is a link or multiple links between the information, your ability to retain and recall information will significantly improve. In summary, linking is a powerful aid to your memory because:

✔ You are preparing information in a way that is more natural to the way patterns are created in your brain.

✔ The use of links in the form of simple lines in your revision notes presents a tremendous opportunity to reduce the number of words but maintain and even increase the level of knowledge transferred.

Use diagrammatic associations to develop a quicker and more holistic understanding of the subject area

✔ You will be amazed how much more knowledge it is possible to include starting with a blank sheet of A4 paper. You are able to write thoughts and ideas in any direction on the piece of paper.

✔ At a glance your mind will not only understand the relationships in a small part of a topic but will appreciate it in the context of the wider subject.

4 Use keywords and therefore use less words

A keyword is a special word used in your revision notes that stimulates or triggers related knowledge specific to the topic or subject you are studying. Using keywords means you will have to read fewer words to understand a specific idea, and therefore you will be able to digest the knowledge more quickly. This is particularly useful when you want to test your knowledge of the spider-diagram during the review sessions.

Keywords are very important if you are to get the best from your revision notes, but it is often very useful to include the phrase or sentence from which that keyword was derived. These words provide reference detail which supports the meaning of the keyword and the key points. This is very valuable during the final stages of revision in ensuring that the keywords and the key points are completely learned.

As you become more familiar with the spider-diagrams, supporting knowledge associated with the keyword is automatically learned

Let us suppose you have excessively summarised your spider-diagram (i.e. you have not included the words that will help you to understand the meaning of the keyword). You can have trouble refamiliarising yourself with the total knowledge contained in a spider-diagram. This is especially true if you have a lot of spider-diagrams to learn.

5 Use hierarchies to prioritise, classify and emphasise the key points

To make your revision notes as easy to learn as possible, and therefore enable you to review your notes rapidly, it is essential to prioritise the knowledge contained in the spider-diagram. There are four simple ways in which you can impose a hierarchy on the keywords and links in order to emphasise the key points:

✔ Use colour to prioritise different grades of keywords and links.

✔ Use different lines and shapes to classify different types of information.

✔ Vary the size of the words or the thickness of the link to reflect its importance.

✔ Use a combination of all of the above.

Colour

Colour coding is a particularly useful technique for prioritising information on the spider-diagram for a later rapid review of the material. Use highlighters to colour code the information very quickly and with minimum fuss. Highlighters come in a range of contrasting colours that will leave a striking impact on the eye. A *possible* hierarchy is described in Figure 8.1.

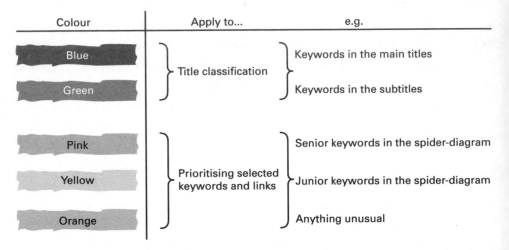

Colour	Apply to...	e.g.
Blue	Title classification	Keywords in the main titles
Green		Keywords in the subtitles
Pink	Prioritising selected keywords and links	Senior keywords in the spider-diagram
Yellow		Junior keywords in the spider-diagram
Orange		Anything unusual

Fig. 8.1
A possible colour hierarchy for prioritising information on spider-diagrams

For very detailed spider-diagrams, classify keywords into senior keywords (highlighted in pink) and junior keywords. The senior keyword is very important during the final stages of revision because at this point you will only need to review the senior keywords to automatically trigger off the knowledge associated with that part of the spider-diagram.

Lines and shapes

Lines and shapes can also be used to replace or reinforce the hierarchy outlined for colour. An example of a line and shape hierarchy is described in Figure 8.2. Alternatively, use the line/shape hierarchy selectively within the colour hierarchy or vice versa. Any combination is possible.

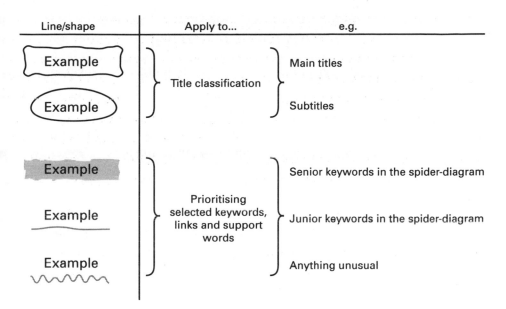

Line/shape	Apply to...	e.g.
Example	Title classification	Main titles
Example		Subtitles
Example	Prioritising selected keywords, links and support words	Senior keywords in the spider-diagram
Example		Junior keywords in the spider-diagram
Example		Anything unusual

Fig. 8.2
A possible line/ shape hierarchy for prioritising information on spider-diagrams

Size of words

Writing small and legibly is an important skill that will enable you to include a lot of very detailed information on a single sheet of paper. This detailed information will be more useful during the earlier reviews when you are cementing your complete understanding of the spider-diagram. You can then skip over this detail during later reviews as you become more familiar with the key points in the spider-diagram.

Writing your spider-diagrams in capital letters will help you to read the information at a higher speed

6 Use position as an aid to memory

Use the openness of spider-diagrams to express your thoughts and ideas in any way or place on the page that pleases you. It will be easier to remember a piece of information when your mind associates it with a particular position on a page.

7 Use exam questions as the focus of the spider-diagram

Having grouped similar past exam questions together (see Chapter 7), place them at the centre or in a very prominent area of the spider-diagram. This will help ensure that all the material included in the spider-diagram is relevant and focused. The spider-diagram should aim to:

1 Provide a complete response to past examination questions.

2 Anticipate answers to future questions through the knowledge you have drawn together from your lecture notes, background reading and all the other original thoughts you have related to the topic.

If you are able to achieve these two aims, all you need to know for the examination is reassuringly contained in the spider-diagram. However, you cannot possibly contain all the information in a spider-diagram to cope with **all** eventualities because you simply have not got the time to learn everything, let alone prepare it.

8 Extend your understanding of the subject in the spider-diagram

A spider-diagram is one of the most profitable ways of tapping into your original thinking because you will have already crystallised your own unique understanding of the subject area from various other sources. New ideas can be easily added to your spider-diagram. Use the freedom you have with a spider-diagram to explore the boundaries of the subject.

9 Spider-diagrams should be a 'one-stop shop' for the final stages of revision

Every effort should be made to maintain a single folder containing all your revision notes. This is a very useful discipline that will help you learn your revision notes quickly during the final stages of revision. If you have a complicated diagram that is not easily summarised within your revision notes, then photocopy it and include it in your folder of revision notes, or paste it directly into your revision notes.

Spider-Diagrams:
Examples

This section provides some illustrative examples of spider-diagrams (Figures 8.7–8.10) which apply the nine principles outlined above. There is no set format for a spider-diagram; therefore any of the illustrative examples should be freely combined and applied to the needs of your subject and your personal learning style.

The example spider-diagrams draw upon extracts which are indicative of past exam questions, lecture notes, background reading and some additional personal thoughts (Figures 8.3–8.6). They reflect – albeit on a very small scale – how the information may be transformed into a spider-diagram.

Fig. 8.3
Past exam questions

Last year's exam
2a) State the three key fats and the effect on blood cholesterol

Penultimate year's exam
2a) Describe the main types of fat and provide examples of each and their properties at room temperature.

Fig. 8.4
Selected passage of lecture notes

Lecture notes on fats
Saturated fats: Hard at room temperature. Found in animal products (meat fat, butter, cream) and in coconut, palm and kernel oils. Intake raises cholesterol.
Polyunsaturated fats: Liquid at room temperature. Oils from vegetable products (sunflower, corn and soyabean). Intake lowers blood cholesterol.
Monounsaturated fats: Olive, peanut and avocado oils. Intake may lower blood cholesterol.

Fig. 8.5
Selected passage of background reading

Selected passage from background reading on diet change and cholesterol
Diet change is the first line of defence against high blood cholesterol. This includes your intake of dietary cholesterol: especially your intake of saturated fats. The American heart association recommends that total fat intake should be restricted to 30% of calories; less than 10% of total calories from saturated fats and no more than 10% of total calories from polyunsaturated fats. The association also recommends that cholesterol intake should be reduced to less than 300mg per day.

Fig. 8.6
Additional thoughts

Some additional personal thoughts having considered the above
People should   1) Select foods with more fish, lean meat and less fatty meats
   2) Eat less fried food and junk food which are high in cholesterol and saturated fats
   3) Eat more fresh fruit and vegetables

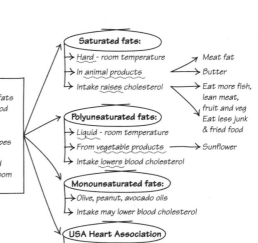

Fig. 8.7
Spider-diagram: Example 1

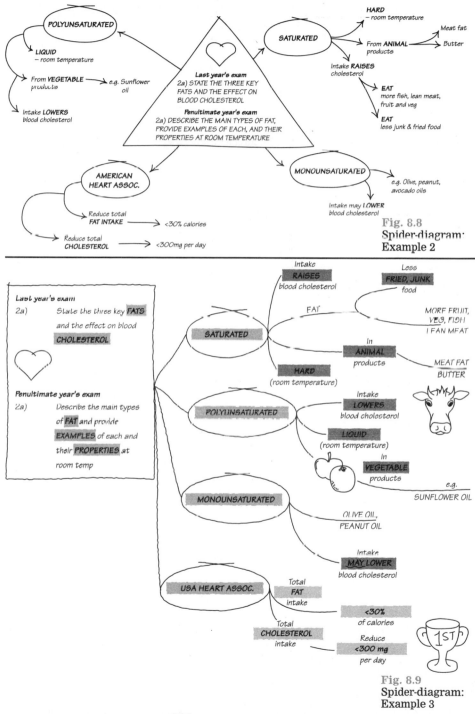

SPIDER-DIAGRAMS

Fig. 8.8
Spider-diagram:
Example 2

Fig. 8.9
Spider-diagram:
Example 3

109

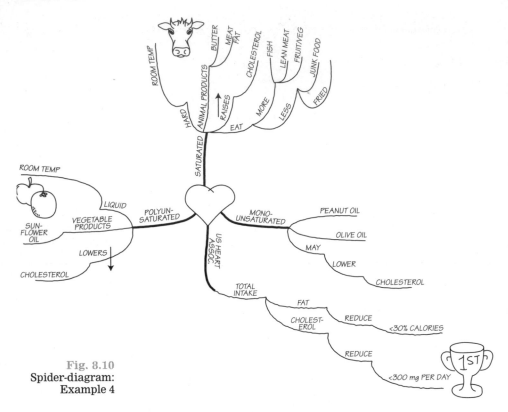

Fig. 8.10
Spider-diagram:
Example 4

Example 4 (Figure 8.10) has many similarities to the Mind Map® approach developed by Tony Buzan, which has influenced the way many people learn. Buzan has also carried out work in areas relating to the potential of the human mind, psychology, memory, speed reading, group study techniques, creativity, and so on. Two books recommended for further reading, both by Tony Buzan, are: *Use Your Head* (BBC Publications, 1975) and *Make the Most of Your Mind* (Pan Books, 1988).

Testing Your Knowledge of the Spider-Diagram

Test yourself constantly

Without a doubt, the technique you use to learn the information arranged in your spider-diagram (or any other form of revision notes) will have the most identifiable effect on your ability to learn. The amount of time you spend trying to learn your spider-diagrams is irrelevant if you are not learning them effectively.

It is not enough simply to read spider-diagrams; you need to test your knowledge to see if you have genuinely digested the material. Simply reading the material is also dangerous because it gives you a false sense of security that you have spent the time studying effectively. If you learn the material in your spider-diagram by combining, reading, thinking, writing and testing, you will be surprised at how little your mind wanders and how much faster you learn.

Push the limits of your learning power

At the time of the final reviews, you are likely to have created quite a number of spider-diagrams and the prospect of having to learn them all will initially be quite frightening.

Firstly, reassure yourself that you have done the hard part in creating a complete and carefully thought-out set of revision notes which contains all the information you need to learn for the exam. Secondly, remind yourself that you are now in a position to know how large or small the task is.

If you know what has to be done you can concentrate on doing it, even if it's a lot. If the total amount to learn on the spider-diagrams seems more than you have ever had to learn before (and it will as you progress through each year at college/university), then each time you will have to summon that extra level of performance from yourself. If you present yourself with daunting learning challenges, providing you know clearly what is to be learned and in what time, you are likely to surpass your own expectations every time.

Learn the spider-diagrams in stages using read and recall

Do not try to absorb the whole spider-diagram into your memory all at once (unless you can). Tackle a little bit of the spider-diagram at a time. Try these alternative approaches:

1 Start by trying to read a small leg of the spider-diagram, then recall that leg in the corresponding place on a blank page. Progress around each leg of the spider-diagram.

2 Read and recall on a blank page the positions of the key headings of the spider-diagram, then read and recall the keywords contained under each of the individual headings.

On each subsequent review you will be able to recall more and more of the spider-diagram and need to read less and less of it. As the exam approaches you will be able to repro-duce the entire spider-diagram on a blank piece of paper from memory with only a quick glance of your spider-diagram.

It is important that you fix the length of your read-and-recall sessions for each spider-diagram in advance. This gives you a specific target time in which to learn the quantity of information contained in the spider-diagram. It is not usually possible to learn a whole spider-diagram completely in (say) five minutes, but the sense of impossibility will somehow induce you to go as far as you can in learning the information contained in the spider-diagram. Such a specific learning target will harness your levels of concentration and you are therefore able to work at the highest possible level of efficiency. Overall, the aim is to read and then re-create as much as possible of each of the spider-diagrams in the time you have allotted.

These read-and-recall sessions should not be taken lightly; plan to re-create conditions as close to the exam room as possible. If you are able to concentrate fully on these read-and-recall sessions, you will be rewarded with a very deep knowledge of your spider-diagram and will have spent less time studying.

Enforce a time limit of ten, five and one minute for each spider-diagram

Set yourself a limit of ten, five and one minute to learn an A4 size spider-diagram. Now let us apply these time limits to the pattern of seven reviews described in Chapter 6:

- ➤ **1st review:**   Preparation of the spider-diagrams.

- ➤ **2nd review:**   Set a limit of ten minutes per spider-diagram.

- ➤ **3rd, 4th, 5th and 6th reviews:**   Set a limit of five minutes per spider-diagram.

- ➤ **24 hours before the exam:**   Set a limit of one minute per spider-diagram to enable you to carry out multiple reviews.

Techniques that help you to learn spider-diagrams more quickly are covered in Chapter 10

Let us suppose you follow the 25-(5)-20-(10) study pattern as discussed in Chapter 5; allowing five minutes to review each spider-diagram, you will be able to review nine spider-diagrams in an hour. Extending this calculation, if you have a total of 23 spider-diagrams for a subject, you know you will be able to review the entire subject in two hours and 25 minutes. It doesn't matter that some spider-diagrams have more information and others have less. It means that in some of these five-minute sessions, you will have to work a little faster.

Now you can see how beautifully easy it is to schedule the learning of your spider-diagrams. You are able to plan very specific objectives in as much detail as every five minutes in the few weeks before the examination. This ensures at this really critical time that you are learning at a very high level of effectiveness.

SUMMARY

This chapter has built upon important points that were developed in earlier chapters and introduced others that are developed in later chapters:

- Chapter 2: If you have fixed your target grade, it will help you to judge what level of detail you require in your spider-diagrams.
- Chapter 5 described an approach to planning the preparation of spider-diagrams and introduced the 25-(5)-20-(10) study pattern, which can be used to schedule the review of your spider-diagrams.
- Chapter 6 described a pattern of review which will ensure that you peak on the day of the exam by planning more frequent reviews of your spider-diagrams as the exam approaches.
- Chapter 7: Spider-diagrams are a synthesis, end product or a coming together as a result of simultaneous consideration of lecture notes, answers to past exam questions, background reading and your own extended understanding of the subject. This will provide you with a deep (and relevant) understanding of the subject.
- Chapter 9 considers how to create mnemonics from keywords used in the spider-diagram to provide an effective memory aid.
- Chapter 10 details an approach to learning spider-diagrams at high speed.

You should now be in a position to:

Prepare your own style of easy-to-learn revision notes

Use pictures, links, keywords and hierarchies to ensure faster mental digestion of information during the final stages of revision

Schedule the learning of your spider-diagrams

Recall all the relevant information at the right level of detail in the examination

Use Mnemonics to Improve Memory During Exams

Mnemonics are highly effective for memorising hundreds of relevant keywords for a group of examinations

Introduction

From the colours of a rainbow to real memory power in an examination

Mnemonics will provide you with an amazing capability to remember long lists of keywords

Mnemonics are widely used by students as a technique for remembering short lists of information, but for many their real potential as an aid to memory remains largely undiscovered. A small number of students really know how to use mnemonics; not surprisingly, these are the ones who regularly do very well in examinations.

Schoolchildren have for many years learned the colours of the rainbow using the mnemonic:

RED ORANGE YELLOW GREEN BLUE INDIGO VIOLET

R O Y G B I V

The colours can be remembered either as the name of a gentleman called 'ROY G. BIV' or using the phrase 'Richard of York Gave Battle In Vain'. In the first case the appropriate keywords are instantly recalled when recollecting a gentleman with a slightly peculiar name.

This chapter extends these simple principles, so that with a little practice you will be confident enough to create and learn mnemonics to store many hundreds of keywords in your short-term memory for a group of exams.

Develop your own mnemonic technique

Mnemonics, like spider-diagrams, are not a 'one-size fits all' study skill. Having read the suggestions put forward in these chapters, adapt and change them to suit your own style, then apply them to situations in which you think you would find them most useful.

There are many uses and variations on the technique of mnemonics. The technique described in this chapter is called the 'story–linkword–keyword' approach and it is superb for quickly remembering a large number of key-words for exams.[1]

Use keyword triggers to help you to plan your answer in the exam

Mnemonics can be used to remember two main types of information: 'lists' and 'linked information using keyword triggers'. There is an important difference, described below:

➤ **Lists**
   If you want to memorise a word in a list, there is no attempt to remember any further information. In the 'rainbow' example above, the only objective is to remember the colours of the rainbow and nothing else about the rainbow.

---

[1] For alternative approaches to mnemonics that include the number–shape, number–rhyme journey method, and the DOMINIC system, see Dominic O'Brien, *How to Pass Exams* (Headline, 1995). This book also contains a good method for learning languages using location, links and imagination.

> **Keyword triggers**
>
> A keyword trigger is a keyword which has been carefully selected from the spider-diagram to trigger off a whole section, branch or network of associated keywords. If you are familiar with your spider-diagrams, a few well-chosen keywords remembered in a mnemonic will help you to elaborate upon all the key points from your spider-diagrams in an exam (see the 'fats' example on page 124 as an illustration of the use of keyword triggers in mnemonics).

If you are new to mnemonics...

If you have not used mnemonics before, the following *very general* rule of thumb may be useful. Let's suppose you are taking a two-hour exam; there should be no difficulty memorising about 100 keywords. This roughly translates into the development of about ten mnemonics, with each of these mnemonics having approximately ten attached keywords.

The 'story–linkword–keyword' technique described in this chapter will enable you to remember a lot more than 100 keywords for every exam, but through careful selection of your keywords this should not be necessary. If the total number of keywords memorised exceeds 150 for every exam, it suggests an overreliance on mnemonics. This can be detrimental to your overall understanding of your revision notes. Remember that mnemonics are useful to **supplement or aid** your memory and understanding, **not to replace** it.

Create a Simple Mnemonic:
Seven Steps

Introduction

The 'story–linkword–keyword' technique can be described in seven steps. Figure 9.1 provides an initial overview of these steps illustrated using keyword triggers from the 'fats' spider-diagram (see Figure 9.2). It is a simple mnemonic example that has only five attached keywords, but it could easily be extended to include many more. Each of the seven steps is described in more detail during the course of this section.

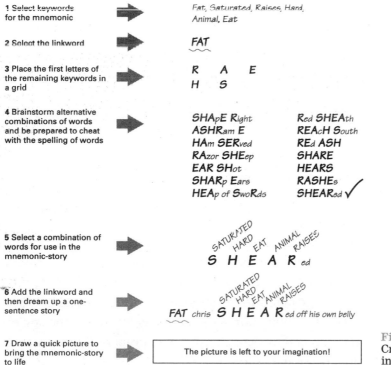

1 Select keywords for the mnemonic

Fat, Saturated, Raises, Hand, Animal, Eat

2 Select the linkword

FAT

3 Place the first letters of the remaining keywords in a grid

R A E
H S

4 Brainstorm alternative combinations of words and be prepared to cheat with the spelling of words

SHApE Right   Red SHEAth
ASHRam E   REAcH South
HAm SERved   REd ASH
RAzor SHEep   SHARE
EAR SHot   HEARS
SHARp Ears   RASHEs
HEAp of SwoRds   SHEARed ✓

5 Select a combination of words for use in the mnemonic-story

SATURATED HARD EAT ANIMAL RAISES
S H E A R ed

6 Add the linkword and then dream up a one-sentence story

SATURATED HARD EAT ANIMAL RAISES
FAT chris S H E A R ed off his own belly

7 Draw a quick picture to bring the mnemonic-story to life

The picture is left to your imagination!

Fig. 9.1
Create a mnemonic in seven steps

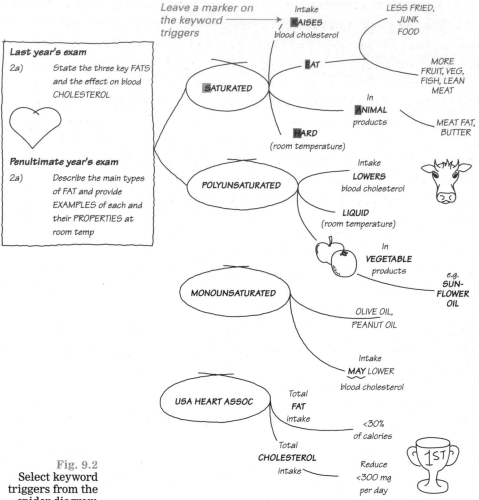

Last year's exam

2a) State the three key FATS and the effect on blood CHOLESTEROL

Penultimate year's exam

2a) Describe the main types of FAT and provide EXAMPLES of each and their PROPERTIES at room temp

Fig. 9.2
Select keyword triggers from the spider-diagram

Where to prepare the mnemonics

Do your 'workings' for the mnemonic opposite the spider-diagram to which it is associated

The best place to prepare a mnemonic is next to the relevant part of your revision notes. If you have a master revision folder that contains all your spider-diagrams, prepare the mnemonic opposite the spider-diagram. This will help you to see the connection between the keywords in the spider-diagram and the workings used to prepare the mnemonic-story (see Figure 9.3).

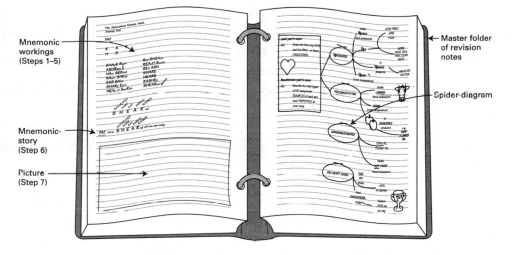

Mnemonic workings (Steps 1–5)

Mnemonic-story (Step 6)

Picture (Step 7)

Master folder of revision notes

Spider-diagram

Step 1: Select keywords for the mnemonic

Fig. 9.3
Preparing mnemonics in close proximity to the revision notes

> **Select keywords that trigger the greatest amount of knowledge**
> The best time to select keywords is about half to two-thirds of the way through the number of reviews you intend to do. At this point you should have achieved a reasonable degree of familiarity with your spider-diagrams.

> **Select unusual keyword triggers from the spider-diagram**
> Choose keywords that are unusual, distinctive or uncommon. You are more likely to remember the associated knowledge contained in the spider-diagram.

Only select a key-word trigger for inclusion in a mnemonic where you really need it to jog your memory

> **Leave a marker on your spider-diagram**
> When you create a mnemonic, you may forget what special association a keyword has with your subject. Mark the keyword selected from the spider-diagrams in some way for future reference (e.g. circle the first letter of the keyword).

➤ **'Fats' example**

My reasons for selecting only five keywords from the 'fats' spider-diagram (see Figures 9.1 and 9.2) to help me to retrieve all the key points depend uniquely on the way my mind creates links between the information contained in the spider-diagram:

1 'Saturated' reminds me that the other keywords selected for inclusion in this mnemonic are related to the properties of saturated fats. I am also aware that the properties of 'Polyunsaturated' fats are in direct contrast to the properties of saturated fats. The information contained under the subheadings of 'Monounsaturated' fats and 'USA Heart Association' are distinctive enough for me to remember without the need for keyword triggers.

2 'Raises' reminds me that saturated fats raise blood pressure and that each of the categories of fats has an effect on blood cholesterol.

3 'Hard' reminds me that saturated fats are hard and that fats can be hard or soft.

4 'Animal' reminds me that saturated fats are based mainly on animal products.

5 'Eat' reminds me that people should eat more or less of certain products.

Step 2: Select the linkword

To help you to remember a large number of mnemonic-stories, you should use a linkword to create an automatic link between the topic area and the mnemonic-story (see Figure 9.4). If the mnemonic-stories are linked to a topic, it is easier to pull out the mnemonic intact from your brain.

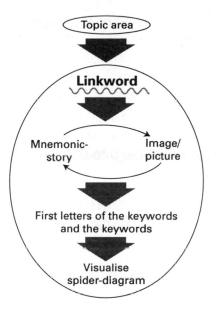

Fig. 9.4
Using the
linkword to
attach the topic
area to the
mnemonic

To make a strong link between the topic area and the mnemonic-story, the linkword should be the only keyword that appears as a whole word in the mnemonic-story (see 'fats' example in Figure 9.1). Furthermore, so that the linkword has a strong affinity with the topic area, select a linkword which is typically a heading/subheading. This will ensure that the mental leap between the topic area and the linkword is a small one.

For example, let us link the mnemonic 'ROY G. BIV' to its topic area. Firstly, select an appropriate linkword, then rewrite the mnemonic in the form of a mnemonic-story (see below).

Use linkwords to help you to remember many, many mnemonics

RED ORANGE YELLOW GREEN BLUE INDIGO VIOLET

ROYG.BIV has a **RAINBOW** coming out of his eyes

Linkword

125

Step 3: Place the first letters of the remaining keywords in a grid

Having decided upon the linkword, place the first letters of the remaining keywords in a grid. This makes it easy to see what combination of words can be developed from the first letters of the keywords (refer to 'fats' example in Figure 9.1).

Step 4: Brainstorm alternative combinations of words and be prepared to cheat with the spelling of words

Use your imagination to dream up an unusual combination of words from the grid (see 'fats' example in Figure 9.1). Quickly write down every combination you can think of, allowing no more than 60 seconds. If you have difficulty creating a combination of words, rearrange the positions of the letters at random in the grid and try again.

Where possible create a combination of words purely from the first letters of the keywords to simplify the mnemonic. An example of this is shown below.

RED ORANGE YELLOW GREEN BLUE INDIGO VIOLET

R O Y G. B I V has a **RAINBOW** coming out of his eyes

A combination of words taken purely from the first letters of the keywords you want to remember

Cheat with the spelling of words if you have difficulty creating a mnemonic-story purely from the first letters of keywords

To quickly create a mnemonic capable of remembering a large number of keywords, you might need to cheat with the spelling of words or use 'support' letters and words to help you to complete a mnemonic-story (see below).

FAT chris S H E A R ed off his own belly

SATURATED HARD EAT ANIMALS RAISES

Cheat with the spelling of words or use 'support' letters if you have to

Use capital letters for those letters and words in the mnemonic-story to which you will attach a keyword, and use lower case for the support letters and words. The fact that you have mixed the cases does not mean the mnemonic-story will be any more difficult to remember, since the spelling and construction of the word will be unusual and distinctive.

Step 5: Select a combination of words for use in the mnemonic-story

Having brainstormed possible combinations of words, select one combination which has the potential to create a memorable one-sentence mnemonic-story (see Figure 9.1).

Step 6: Add the linkword and then dream up a one-sentence story

Having identified a combination of words and separated the linkword, you are now ready to let your imagination run wild and complete a one-sentence mnemonic-story (see Figure 9.1).

Make sure that at least one person is featured in the story. It could be a friend, lecturer, someone you have seen around, someone you like/dislike, a famous person, a family member, etc. If that person is doing something unusual, or something unusual is happening to them, that will help to make the mnemonic-story all the more memorable! The use of colourful, outrageous, obscene, violent and sexual language in the mnemonic-story is particularly effective. In summary, if you can't remember your mnemonic-story, your story was not outrageous enough.

Step 7: Draw a quick picture to bring the mnemonic-story to life

Pictures are a great way of embedding the mnemonic-story in the mind and you can have a little fun while creating them. The pictures do not have to be very detailed; a quick sketch will suffice. Use colour where possible in the sketch and the background to create a strong, bright and vivid image. Where you have used people in the mnemonic-story, try to include exaggerated facial expressions that reflect their part in the mnemonic-story.

Learning Mnemonic-Stories for the Exam

Learn the mnemonic-stories at speed

These mnemonic-stories will only ever be useful for the one exam and consequently you will only need to commit them to your short-term memory. The ideal time to learn the mnemonic-stories is in the few days (and particularly the 24 hours) before the exams. Therefore, you will need to learn them quickly. It should take no more than three 30-minute sessions to memorise approximately ten mnemonic-stories (about 100 keywords) for each subject.

After having created a master sheet of all mnemonic-stories for each subject (see Figure 9.5), the key steps for learning all the mnemonic-stories are as follows:

1 On a blank sheet of paper practise writing out the first mnemonic-story until it is learned.

2 Practise writing out the second mnemonic-story until it is learned.

3 Check that the first mnemonic-story was actually learned.

4 Practise writing out the third mnemonic-story until it is learned.

5 Check that the second mnemonic-story was actually learned, etc.

When you have reached the end of the master sheet, practise writing out the mnemonic-stories for the whole subject.

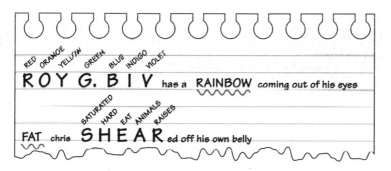

RED ORANGE YELLOW GREEN BLUE INDIGO VIOLET

R O Y G. B I V has a RAINBOW coming out of his eyes

SATURATED HARD EAT ANIMALS RAISES

FAT chris S H E A R ed off his own belly

Fig. 9.5
Create a master sheet of all the mnemonic-stories for a subject

Re-creating mnemonics in the exam

The sequence of events for re-creating a mnemonic in an exam situation is as follows. On reading the question, you should be reminded of your chosen linkword and the mnemonic-story. Write out the mnemonic-story on a corner of the exam question paper and then fill in the keywords. As you glance through the keywords in the mnemonic-story, all the carefully prepared detail contained in your spider-diagram should spring to your mind (see Figure 9.6).

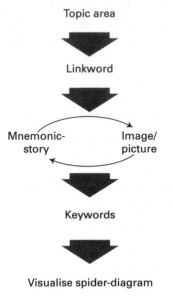

Topic area

Linkword

Mnemonic-story ⟷ Image/picture

Keywords

Visualise spider-diagram

Types of fats and effects on cholesterol

FAT

FAT chris **S H E A R**ed off his own belly

FAT chris **S H E A R**ed off his own belly
(SATURATED, HARD, EAT, ANIMALS, RAISES)

Recollect detail derived from lecture notes, background reading, answers to past exams and extended understanding of the subject

Fig. 9.6
Re-create the mnemonic in an exam

Mnemonics:
A Variation

We will end this chapter by looking at a variation of the 'story–linkword–keyword' mnemonic technique. In this example, the first letter of every keyword has a **sister** word which is used to create a mnemonic-story. The mnemonic-story might now read 'Fat Ronald Affectionately Smells Hillary Everyday' (see below).

The advantage is that the mnemonic is easier to remember because, with the exception of the linkword, every letter in the story has a keyword attached to it. The disadvantage is

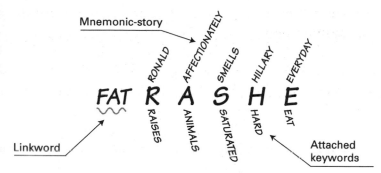

that the stories will be longer if you need to remember many keywords.

If you have any difficulty remembering the attached keyword from the first letters, use your imagination to visually link each keyword with each word from the mnemonic-story to create five unforgettable vivid mental images:

1 Ronald–Raises   4 Hillary Hard

2 Affectionately–Animals   5 Everyday–Eat

3 Smells–Saturated

SUMMARY

You are now in a position to...

Carefully select keywords for inclusion in a mnemonic

Use linkwords to attach the mnemonic to a topic area

Create a one-sentence mnemonic-story

Use mnemonics to jog your memory in the examinations

Rapid Revision

The 24 hours before an exam are critical.
Multiple rapid reviews carried out in the 24
hours before the exam will ensure that you
maximise the use of your short-term memory
and peak on the day of the exam

High-Speed Learning in the 24 Hours Before an Exam

The three skills of rapid revision

Apply special learning techniques for the 24 hours before an exam and it will be possible to take yourself through a steep learning curve that will give you great confidence for the exam. Three interrelated skills describe the 'rapid revision' approach put forward in this chapter:

1   Take full advantage of your instinctively high level of concentration in the 24 hours before an examination by setting yourself more demanding revision tasks. Familiarity with the revision notes will enable you to cut down sharply on the time limit you allow to review every spider-diagram.

2   Engage and harmonise as many senses as possible during the review.

3   Use a shorthand writing technique.

Place an aggressive limit on the time allowed to review each spider-diagram

Limit the time allowed to review a spider-diagram to two minutes, then to one minute

In Chapter 8 a limit of ten, five and one minute was suggested as the time allowed to review each spider-diagram. During the 24 hours before an exam you should have attained a sufficient level of knowledge to limit the time for reviewing each spider-diagram to as little as one minute.

Carrying out reviews within this aggressive time limit will unquestionably be a very demanding activity. But on the day before an exam you should have little difficulty producing the required level of concentration. Furthermore, if you really believe that you can absorb all the information you need to during a rapid review, it will be possible. To help you complete a rapid review of a spider-diagram, apply 'three-sense revision' and 'learn by scribble' as described below.

'Three-sense revision'

Chapter 8 described an approach to learning spider-diagrams in stages, first by reading, then by recalling them. This structured approach will help you to build a strong understanding and a competent recall of your revision notes. In the 24 hours before an exam, the aim is quite simply to soak up as much information as possible into your short-term memory in the shortest possible time. As you will be able to push yourself a little harder at this time, you should therefore follow a different approach to learning your revision notes.

If you can simultaneously review your revision notes using 'multiple senses', information will be more quickly absorbed and more deeply embedded into the short-term memory. This is because you are exercising more of your brain when you process the knowledge through your mind and body in as many ways as possible. In practice, this means that you read your notes, write your notes and whisper your revision notes all at the same time (see Figure 10.1).

Enhance your ability to absorb information in the final 24 hours by reading, writing and whispering your revision notes all at the same time

You may know of a place to study when no one else will be there, e.g. a research lab or lecture room in the evenings. Consider singing or shouting your revision notes in an unusual way. It will be very embarrassing if anyone hears you, but if used every now and then, a surprising amount of information can be made to stick in the mind!

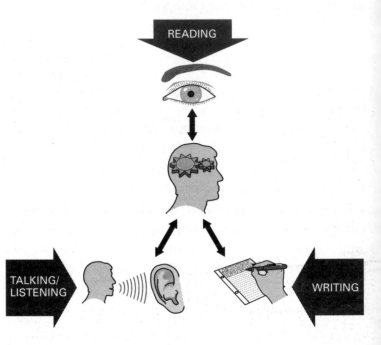

Fig. 10.1
'Three-sense revision'

Learn by scribble

Writing out your revision notes is an important part of learning them quickly. The benefit of writing out revision notes is that you digest the information through more senses. This helps you to focus your mind and hence avoid daydreaming.

Use 'learn by scribble' to write information at a pace which more closely matches the pace at which your mind works

The problem is that your writing speed is likely to be slower than your reading speed and your whispering/listening speed. In addition, your writing speed will certainly be much slower than your thinking speed. Therefore, if you can increase the speed at which you rewrite your revision notes, your overall revision speed will be much higher.

In this section, we look at an abbreviated form of writing that will take you through all the benefits of writing out your revision notes, but in much less time. Let us consider what happens when people write out their signatures. The faster a signature is written, the less likely it is that the signature will resemble the original letters, but the signatory will still feel as if they have written their name (see Figure 10.2).

Let us extend this very simple principle to rewriting your revision notes (see Figure 10.3). The result will be a page of scribbles written at high speed. It does not matter how messy your *rewritten* revision notes are because you will never have to read them again. The most important thing is that your mind has processed the information.

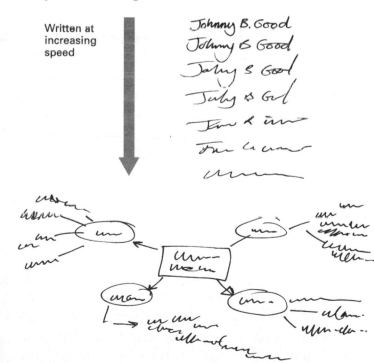

Written at increasing speed

Fig. 10.2
Using a signature as an example of writing at speed

Fig. 10.3
Using 'learn by scribble' to rewrite a spider-diagram

Late-Night Revision

Use late-night revision selectively

Late-night revision
can be very helpful
but use it selectively

There is a saying that if you don't know your 'stuff' the night before an exam, you never will. This is completely untrue: if you don't know it yet, you still have the whole night to learn it! If you have an exam at 9am, you have up to 8–12 hours available during a late-night revision session. There are times when late-night revision is quite simply a necessary evil. The best-laid plans can go awry, so you should know how to deal with a late-night session if, as a last resort, you need to go through one.

When you have the pressure of an exam the next day, this may be the one time that your mind and body are able to cope with a late-night session without too much difficulty. Now, a word of caution. If you use late-night sessions too frequently, your normal pattern of sleep will be completely disturbed. The result will be tiredness and a drop in your overall performance, so use them only in **emergencies**.

Energy foods

Your intake of energy foods can have an important effect on your 'study stamina' during a late-night revision session. A large quantity of chocolate, glucose tablets or a can of Lucozade can work wonders. Eat and drink a little bit at 10–15-minute intervals to keep your level of energy and your level of performance as high as possible. Make sure you are well stocked up with chocolate during the exam period. You'll have plenty of time to work off any overindulgence after the exam. An alter-native to energy foods are light exercises or stretches. If you can help the flow of blood around your brain and body, you'll feel more alert.

SUMMARY

You are now in a position to...

Capitalise on the inevitable pressure in the 24 hours before an exam

Place aggressive limits on the time allowed to carry out a review

Simultaneously use multiple senses during a review

Significantly improve upon the speed at which your revision notes are rewritten

Carry out a late-night revision session if appropriate

Perform rapid multiple reviews in the 24 hours before an exam

The
Exam

Do not let your hard work go to waste. Know how to prepare for the exam and how to tackle it

Teamwork

Share knowledge within a study clique

Helping and receiving help from a small group of friends you know well can be enormously helpful. This is especially true if you have developed a feeling of trust between you rather than one of mutual suspicion and fear that others are trying to exploit your work.

Study cliques are valuable for testing and expanding your knowledge in a subject area in a way that is very different to private study. Meeting with your study group at fixed times will discipline you to make the best use of your study hours. Study groups are also a useful forum for tackling difficult problems and subject areas that did not receive adequate explanation in the lecture:

✔ You are more likely to remember how to tackle a tricky exam question if it was discussed with friends.

✔ Working through difficult problems on your own can mean hours of frustration, which saps your motivation.

✔ Discussing difficult areas can be a great way to let off steam. It is reassuring to know that you are not alone and that others have similar difficulties.

✔ It helps you to prioritise areas for further private study.

✔ It is always useful to get another person's interpretation or understanding of the study material.

✔ A friend may have picked up a vital piece of understanding that you may have missed.

Help your classmates

Providing assistance to your classmates could mean giving away inside information you have on likely exam questions or helping someone to tackle a problem for which you have found a shortcut. Unfortunately, some degree courses have developed a culture (especially where ranking is important to degree classification) in which students are reluctant to provide others with genuine help and advice for fear that they might be helping a potential competitor. This can be counterproductive. Help others where possible and you will actually develop and test your own understanding.

Before the Exam

Planning time around the exams

However badly you have planned or organised yourself in the weeks before the exam, the days just before and in between the exams provide you with a last opportunity to redeem yourself. Even if you have prepared thoroughly for the exams, effective planning around exam time is still essential to ensure that you peak at the highest level possible.

Fill out your daily planner for the whole of the exam period (see Chapter 5). Always be aware of exactly how many reviews you intend to fit in before the exam. For example, if you know you have only two reviews left per subject, you will automatically raise your level of concentration to ensure that you learn the material during these two reviews (see Chapter 6).

Panic only about your next exam

Make sure that the early exams go well so that you build up your confidence for the later exams. The worry is that in the days before an exam you will have many subjects you feel you need to revise. Don't panic about all the exams all at once. Panic only about one exam at a time, and that should be your next exam. It is much more productive to panic in this way.

Last-minute mental preparation

Just as athletes need to focus themselves in the minutes before the race, you too should find an activity which mentally prepares you for your examination. Try any of the following suggestions:

- ✔ Avoid all classmates who talk about their last-minute anxieties!

- ✔ Talk to your classmates and share last-minute anxieties!

- ✔ Listen to a particularly calming/rousing piece of music.

- ✔ Say a prayer.

Eat chocolate

There are few times in one's life when chocolate can be eaten without any guilt whatsoever. This is one of them. To avoid tiredness in the exam, eat as much chocolate as you can (without feeling sick). I strongly recommend that you consume large quantities of chocolate at the following intervals before the exam:

Do not underestimate the benefits of chocolate on exam performance

- ✔ 2 hours
- ✔ 1 hour
- ✔ 10 minutes

Have an exam partner

For morning exams, take the precaution of asking an exam partner (classmate) to knock on your door or telephone you, and agree to do the same for your classmate. If you had a late night, you may have overslept or even forgotten to set your alarm clock. An exam partner will also reassure you that you are going to the right place at the right time.

Double-check the time and location of all your exams at least a week before they begin

Record your revision notes

A great way to learn your revision notes (especially when there is only a little time between the exams) is to play them back on a personal stereo. This is an alternative to working through a set of revision notes and is much less strenuous. Listening to your own voice will help you relax, and the information will subliminally sink into your mind and help you focus on the next exam with ease!

During the Exam

Reading the question

Do more than simply read the exam question before attempting to answer it. Highlight, underline or circle the important keywords of the question that will help you to make sure that you have fully understood it. Do not let all your hard work be wasted by answering something slightly different.

When reading and picking out important keywords from the exam question, pay particular attention to words such as 'describe', 'express', 'draw on', 'show', 'discuss', 'outline' or 'state'. They tell you the level of detail required in the answer.

Let us suppose that you have read the question properly and you cannot give the examiners exactly what they want. **Creatively link** ideas to points you think they want you to make or think that you might be able to get away with. Most examiners will expect more than a simple regurgitation of lecture notes in your answers. Therefore creative linking of your ideas and knowing how to apply the information you have to the exam question are very important skills.

Planning an answer

Always take a few moments to plan your answer on a rough piece of paper. Jot down the key points from your understanding, and/or the keywords from a mnemonic and/or part of a spider-diagram. This will help you to structure your answer and ensure that it covers all the key areas in the available time.

Answer layouts

In laying out your answer to the exam question, help the examiner to find the key points you know they are looking for. For example, underline important words, and number and space out your answer.

Make sure you know the style of answer each of your examiners expects from you (see also Chapter 3). If there are shortcuts you can use to convey the message more quickly, use them, but be aware that there are certain types of shortcuts that annoy examiners:

- Freehand sketches as opposed to diagrams drawn with a ruler.
- Answers in the form of bullet points as opposed to answers written in full sentences.
- Reproduction of the lecture notes as opposed to the application of the principles outlined in the lecture notes.

After an exam

The time between exams is often very short. Having just completed an exhausting exam, the last thing you want to do is have to revise for the next one. Therefore, it is very important to have planned what revision you need to do between the exams before you begin a group of exams.

If your motivation drops, visualise the things you hope to do when all the exams are over. If you feel an exam did not go too well, turn your attention to the next exam. Do not dwell on what cannot be changed.

After All of the Exams

When all the exams are over, some people suffer from mental torture and hallucinations. Small errors made in an exam convince them they have done a lot worse than was actually the case. Forget the exams after you have finished them. Have a few drinks to flush all those exam stresses out of your system.

SUMMARY

You are now in a position to...

Share information around the time of the exam

Prepare for the exam

Perform well in the exam

Relax after the exam

Projects and Dissertations

During your degree, you might be required to do an extended piece of coursework, project, dissertation or a thesis. No matter how successful the results of your project, you will not be doing justice to your efforts unless you can write up your research, analysis and findings effectively

Introduction

The end of a project is where you choose the end to be

A word of caution. Projects are open-ended exercises. It is possible to spend years doing a piece of project work and still have unanswered questions at the end of it. Where the write-up is the major piece of evidence on which your contributions are judged, there comes a point when you are better off using your time to write up the analysis you have already carried out rather than doing more reading and more experiments. There is a fine line between spending too much time doing the analysis and not leaving enough time to write it up.

Always begin with the end in mind

Make sure you have an outline for your write-up at the earliest stage of the project. You need to fit the pieces of the 'jigsaw' together as soon as they are available, otherwise you may realise too late where you really needed to direct your efforts in order to complete your findings and your write-up.

Objectives: Get the balance right and be focused

There are two suggestions you should bear in mind when agreeing the objectives of the project with your supervisor. Firstly, it is important to agree the *extent* of your objectives for the project. Of course you want to set yourself challenging targets, but it is worse to disappoint, and better to exceed expectations. This is a difficult balance to achieve.

Secondly, at whatever level you choose to pitch the difficulty of the project, eliminate ambiguity concerning the objectives of the project. If a project has a vague objective (i.e. is not focused), it is much more difficult to target your work during the project, and it is even more difficult for the lecturer to judge your work against these objectives during the write-up.

Structure your approach to writing

For some people writing comes so naturally that it is completed in one single effort with neither much planning nor editing. Unless you fall into this category, you will find it helpful to follow a structured approach when writing your project. A three-stage approach is outlined below and described in more detail during the course of this chapter:

1 Develop a table of contents.

2 Organise and collect the information in a way that will help you to manage and write up the project.

3 Write or type the first draft of each chapter after reviewing all the information relating to that chapter. Then edit the drafts until completion.

Develop a Table of Contents

The first step when writing up a project is to develop a table of contents in as much detail as possible. A well-thought-out table of contents provides a structure and a plan of action that should keep you 'on track' for the duration of the project.

Brainstorm the key areas

A useful way to brainstorm the various sub-sections that make up your table of contents is to create a spider-diagram. It is a good method of looking at interrelationships between different areas of the project and exploring new and fruitful areas for research, analysis and investigation based upon your original thoughts on the subject. The key message here is to be prepared to examine different ways of potentially organising the material and not to expect to write or type a perfect table of contents the first time around.

Break the table of contents into smaller, logical sections which flow from one subheading to another

Structure your work using a table of contents at the earliest stage. This will save you time because it will force you to think about the finished argument when it is easiest to change it

The best chance that you have to structure the logic and flow of your argument is during the preparation of the table of contents. If you properly apply yourself to this task you will save yourself much time and agony. Later, during the writing phase, you will avoid having to rewrite sections that do not fit within the structure or, worse, having to throw away sections you do not need.

If you can break down the project into smaller, more manageable blocks of writing, the writing of the project will seem much less daunting. Furthermore, it is easier to schedule how long you can afford to spend writing up each sub-section and when you should do it.

The table of contents is your master plan, but don't be afraid to change it. Clearly number all the levels and keep all headings/subheadings as specific as possible. Copy it out neatly (or type it out) and put it somewhere where you can quickly refer to it.

Logbooks

Having created a table of contents, keep two logbooks to help you to manage your project. The first logbook is paper-based and contains the administration and organisation of the project.

The second logbook can either be paper-based or electronic and it contains the headings from your table of contents spaced evenly throughout its pages. Under these headings collect your notes and ideas; these will become invaluable to you during the write-up. Both logbooks are discussed in more detail below.

The 'administration' logbook

If you effectively organise and record information in your logbook, your mind will not be overly occupied with the administration of the project and will be free to tackle the difficult problems. The administration logbook may typically contain:

If you look organised, you will feel organised and be organised

- Plans and schedules.

- Interview notes.

- Notes of meetings with supervisors.

- Experimental or empirical analysis.

- Lists of actions (problems, queries, people you need to see, texts you need to obtain, phone calls you need to make, etc.).

Lecturers are particularly fussy about the inclusion of accurate references in project work

✔ Lists of literature searches and references. Always make a full record of every reference just after you have read a piece of literature. A few moments' effort will later save you many wasted hours hunting for a reference when the deadline is almost upon you. Set aside a few pages at the back of the logbook to record these references.

During the course of a project you will record many valuable entries in your logbook. Unless these entries are clearly laid out, well presented and easy to find, you may not be bothered to refer to it. As a consequence, important details will get overlooked. Apply the following good practice suggestions to your logbook:

✔ Clearly title and date each entry.

✔ Grade the importance of the entries and key points made in your logbook using highlighter pens for quick reference during the write-up.

✔ Number all the pages of the logbook.

✔ In the event of losing your logbook, write your name, address and telephone number on the inside front cover of the logbook.

Logbooks do not always come equipped with margins, giving you the flexibility to choose a layout for your logbook which you find comfortable. When making an entry in a logbook, make quick notes that are legible, easy to find and do not need rewriting. My preference for the administration logbook is for each page to be divided into two halves, with margins in both halves (see Figure 12.1). This is a very useful format for recording entries in which you can prepare questions or identify issues that require a response on the right-hand side of the page, for example meetings with supervisors, telephone interviews, etc.

In the sample layout of an administration logbook shown in Figure 12.1, a method for monitoring 'actions' is described. All the actions are identified by a triangular symbol. On completion, a tick is placed at the centre of the triangle.

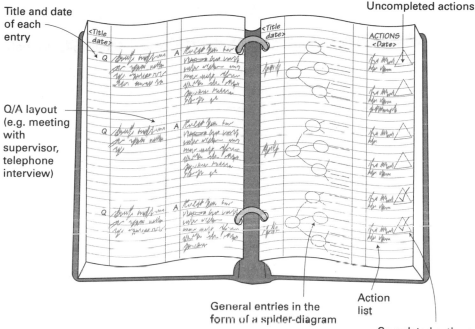

Title and date of each entry

Uncompleted actions

Q/A layout (e.g. meeting with supervisor, telephone interview)

General entries in the form of a spider-diagram

Action list

Completed actions

The 'ideas and write-up' logbook

As outlined earlier, the second logbook is an ongoing and orderly collection of all your notes and ideas which will be very helpful to you when you begin to write the first draft. A number of pages are set aside for every heading/subheading from the table of contents. Whenever you have a surge of inspiration related to any aspect of your project, you have a 'home' in your logbook where you can collect such ideas. If this is postponed, surges of inspiration are forgotten or are not captured as eloquently as when they are fresh in the mind. Under each of the subheadings you may also wish to:

Fig. 12.1
Two sample pages from an administration logbook

✔ Explore or record ideas.

✔ Make summary notes from important articles/books.

✔ Collect material for ready inclusion in the write-up, e.g. sketches and diagrams.

✔ Begin to draft difficult parts of the write-up.

If you have chosen to use a paper-based logbook, we shall again return to the advantages of using spider-diagrams. They are an excellent way to record information under a subheading, because you can:

✔ Jot down a lot of thoughts very quickly and see the connection between them.

✔ Add to spider-diagrams very easily without making a mess of your existing notes.

✔ Quickly refamiliarise yourself with the ideas at a later date.

There is one further valuable home for your project information. Keep all the other support documents related to your project in a loose-leaf A4 file. Examples include department guidelines, relevant articles, photocopies from books, pictures, graphs, copies of chapter drafts, etc. Where possible information should be collected under each chapter number.

Writing the Draft

Planning the write-up: Schedule a fixed writing task every day

Writing up a project will unquestionably test your time management skills to the limit. Editing drafts, producing clear diagrams, completing references, writing an abstract, proofreading, reflecting the comments of your supervisor on early drafts, making copies of final scripts, etc. will all take much longer than you can possibly imagine.

When planning the write-up look through your table of contents. Allocate the subheadings into small (manageable) daily writing tasks. This will then indicate to you how long you need to complete the write-up.

So, unless you enjoy very little sleep approaching the deadline:

✔ Start writing early.

✔ Maintain a feeling of daily positive achievement and schedule a fixed writing task every day.

✔ Set interim deadlines to complete specific writing targets, and stick to them.

✔ Be generous with blank time (or catch-up time). Unexpected things will happen, and some things will always go wrong.

✔ Write up earlier chapters in parallel to the ongoing work related to the project.

Review the material associated with a chapter then write the draft for that chapter

There are two parts to writing the first draft of a chapter. You should review the relevant material (it is very easy to be lazy at this point) before you write it. Far too many students begin writing drafts without properly reviewing the material they have worked so hard to discover and collect.

Having already collected your preliminary thoughts and ideas in the 'write-up' logbook, glance over the material under the subheadings of the chapter you are about to write. Add any further points you think you should include in the write-up. Then briefly reread any key pages or documents from your administration logbook and your loose-leaf A4 file.

The aim is to quickly 'load up' your **short-term memory** with all information related to one chapter, then to capture all that knowledge in the form of either a handwritten or typed draft chapter. A two-part approach such as this will ensure that your facts are correct, the logic is consistent and that the argument flows. It also means there is less wasted effort in rewriting the draft.

Maintain the writing flow

There are times when you need to look at the whole to see where real adjustments to the detail are required

To meet your deadlines, it is important not to get too 'bogged down' on a tricky part of the write-up and maintain the writing flow. Just leave a marker in the text (e.g. an asterisk) so that you can return to it at a later date and tackle it with a fresh perspective.

During the electronic editing process there will also be occasions when ideas do not seem to fit the argument you are developing in that chapter, yet you do not feel brave enough to delete material because you may want to rework it or use it in a different part of the write-up. To maintain the writing flow in such cases, set up a 'junk' file and cut and paste these ideas into this temporary store.

Computer disasters

It is incredibly annoying and painful to have lost your write-up approaching a critical deadline. Don't ever think that your files on hard drives or floppy disks are infallible. Files can get corrupted and accidentally deleted, and disks can get lost and damaged. Take the precautions of having a copy of your file on a hard drive and on a floppy disk. Regularly rename these files (e.g. Chapter _1a, 1b…) and print off the occasional hard copy.

The following list is not meant to frighten you, but when you are chasing a deadline, and especially when you are at the mercy of the available computer resources at your university, expect the worst. You will need to allow for unimaginable surges in demand for computers, printer jams, printer breakdowns, inconceivably long print queues, paper shortages, ink cartridges running dry, virus alerts, network maintenance and network breakdowns.

SUMMARY

You are now in a position to...

Develop a table of contents that is equivalent to a 'writing'
plan of action

Use two logbooks and a file to manage all the information related to
the project

Use your short-term memory to write the first draft of each chapter

Carry out the writing in small, manageable chunks

Understand that the write-up is the major piece of evidence on which
your efforts are judged

Final Remarks

Never forget that your aim is to achieve the maximum grade for the minimum amount of effort. The Total Learning approach directs you to the skills that can really make a difference to your performance. Begin by making small and steady improvements to your learning technique, and you will shatter the myth that to do extremely well you have to be a 'swot'. Best of luck.

Index